ARCHITECT THAT

BUILDING YOUR BUSINESS BY LEADING FROM THE BOTTOM UP

TRAVIS FOX

ARCHITECT THAT
Building your business by leading from the bottom up

iUniverse books may be ordered through booksellers or by contacting:

iUniverse
1663 Liberty Drive
Bloomington, IN 47403
www.iuniverse.com
1-800-Authors (1-800-288-4677)

Because of the dynamic nature of the Internet, any web addresses or links contained in this book may have changed since publication and may no longer be valid. The views expressed in this work are solely those of the author and do not necessarily reflect the views of the publisher, and the publisher hereby disclaims any responsibility for them.

Any people depicted in stock imagery provided by Thinkstock are models, and such images are being used for illustrative purposes only. Certain stock imagery © Thinkstock.

ISBN: 978-1-5320-2492-4 (sc)
ISBN: 978-1-5320-2493-1 (e)

Print information available on the last page.

iUniverse rev. date: 06/12/2018

DEDICATION

To those who seek to bring their authentic selves
to their business and those they serve.
Conscious companies going heart forward into
a worldwide audience, may this be a first and /
or larger step into your next adventure.
Thank you to those who have taught guided and
helped me become the Architect of my Being.

PREFACE

You are about to journey into a new way of leading yourself and your team through today's corporate infrastructure and worldwide marketplace, welcome reader.

This book is based on the five-week trainings I have been doing for the last twenty years over my career to private corporations, while not releasing this information or process publically. After a brief retirement to spend time with family and my own personal development around the globe, you are beginning your journey contained within these pages to Architect your business and somewhat self.

The approach I have found best taken, is to take it literally like you were at one of our live events. That meaning take each chapter digest it and re-read. Then take the five-week experience, as did the group that went through it from which these pages are written. In clarity, chapter one becomes week one for the process, coaching, Architecting and homework to fully ingest the teachings here, chapter over chapter and week over week. From then watch how your business grows both internally and externally, while revisiting the areas you see still need deeper Architecting.

We look forward to hearing about your successes and with each company changing their approach to building their businesses. You can reach us at www.TravisFox.net to schedule Architect in

Training (AIT) interview, online support and of course one-to-one Architecting.

Thank you for being willing to realize that change is constant and we are constantly changing. By your decision to change your mind you literally change yourself, your company, your team and the world of business.

See you one the other side.

Travis Fox,
Architect of Being

CHAPTER # 1

Architecting360 Training I

(Strong, and Confident)

Introduction

I think it's important to consider why you are reading this book, so let me lay it out for you. My primary goal is to help people fix themselves. This book is about one thing: the people *inside* people. You, as many others do, likely believe that you have to push past your old habits to make changes, and if you've done this before, you know how challenging it can be. This tends to be problematic for most people because there are psychological ramifications as to why and what stops those changes from happening. If we could minimize that gap of understanding and time, imagine how much more exciting life would be.

First of all, I congratulate you for being willing to do something different, because it is quite easy to do the same thing over and over again and still expect a different result. You probably deal with that every day; as do I. Our world has become static and habitual. It's time to break these habits, which may not even be yours by choice. It's time to change into the human awareness and go beyond what you were taught, and to know what you were built to do. Most importantly.... to *BE*.

If I came up to you and told you that you were insane and needed therapy, would you sign up? It's a rhetorical question; so don't bother answering (but you knew that). It simply doesn't work that way. When you're in psych school they say, "Don't worry, word of mouth will get you business." That is completely false. Again, it doesn't work that way. So, instead of making the mountain come to us, so-to-speak, we just... went to the mountain. We created a series of networks to allow others to find their own path — their own inner psychologist. Here we are twenty-five years later, and we've developed a new system for Guided Self-Discovery for Freedom, and I mean **FREEDOM**. I'll explain what that means a little bit later.

I'll tell you upfront that there is a spiritual overtone to everything that I do, I'm not trying to hide that, but I'm not here to preach. I'm not interested in whether you're Jewish, Christian, Buddhist, Muslim, Daoist/Taoist, Anarchist, Nihilist, Jedi, Team Jacob, whatever... Doesn't matter. I'm frankly not educated enough to expound on the virtues of various religions or try to sway your spiritual beliefs, but I will ask you to agree on one thing: Very simply, all of us have a date with eternity. How you choose to get there is up to you, but make no mistake, you *are* going to get there. Now, do we all agree on that? Look, I don't want to offend anybody, but in all likelihood, I probably will. I'm okay with that. I'm not here to tell you what to believe. That's just not my style. You need to discover those things for yourself—hence "Guided Self-Discovery"—because I can't be guiding you all the time. To be honest, you wouldn't want me to. You'd get sick of that *real* fast.

What I'm offering here are the first five steps of a larger program, and although it's a shortened version, there's more than a meal here, if you know what I mean. The deeper program is called "Finding Out Who You Are Not - A Path to I AM." We're going to start simple, and in some ways, you're my new Guinea pigs. Luckily, though, this isn't our first rodeo. We've ironed out all the kinks, so you'll be much further ahead when all is said and done.

HyPerformanceTM Relaxation:

Slight brief: I always like to start with something a little fun by asking people to question certain things. I'm not going to lie, it's almost purely for my own entertainment, but still, bear with me here. Now, this game has rewards. It also has rules, and you need to know them. I'm going to ask you four questions, and you have a limited amount of time to answer. Of course, you'll have to time yourself, because if you haven't noticed, I'm not sitting in front of you with a stopwatch. And if I am... that's a super weird coincidence. Anyway, you've got ten seconds to answer, so think quick. If you don't get the answer, I am in no way obligated to tell it to you. I *might*... if I'm in a good mood, but I am *not* obligated. Got it? Good. Let's Begin:

1. Who was Tiger Woods' first golf instructor?

You guessed, don't lie. The answer to this first question is Earl Woods. There you go. If you got it right, well done. Good job. Here's the part in the live show where you'd get a prize, a CD or Download. But you're not at the live show, are you? No prize for you.

Increase your self-confidence

The second question is meant to help increase your self-confidence and self-esteem, and it's usually more effective if we're in the same room, but let's go ahead with it anyway.

2. Who is the defending Master Champion?

Assuming you're a golfer, you would know, that at the time of this writing, the answer is Patrick Reed. If you're more of a bowler, you wouldn't. Do you feel that? That's the stakes getting higher. Get ready.

3. Who was Einstein's first-grade teacher?

You were almost certainly wrong. And you know what? I'm not going to tell you the answer because I don't have to. That was always an option from the start, remember? Google it or something, It doesn't matter.

Ok, let's kick things up a notch. Imagine you're playing this game live with me and in front of a crowd. Oh, and there's $100 on the line. *Feel* the pressure, don't you.

4. Who was Bach's first piano instructor?

Usually when I ask this question, there's nothing but silence as the attendees rack their brains for an answer...

Well thanks for playing.

Now let's look at what was really happening versus what you most likely *thought* was happening. When you take a closer look, you'll notice a theme or pattern within those questions. Patterns are what makes the world go 'round, especially when concerning we humans and how we interact with our worlds, both internal and external. Patterns can be and often are a wonderful thing to behold, but when we have patterns that we can't seem to break or modify, they become our worst enemy. By the end of this book, you will have the tools to identify, verify, and modify any pattern in your world, and truly change your life from the inside out.

So, did you catch the theme? All great minds, be them the minds of performers, athletes, corporate juggernauts, etc., ... all of them throughout history have had one thing in common: They had a COACH who guided them and helped them reach their fullest potential. That is what I do. I'm not saying I'm perfect (believe me, I'm not!), but I am saying that I can help you. It's my job to help you figure out *who you are,* because if you're going to be stuck with yourself 24/7, you'd better be able to like yourself.

That's what I am. I'm a Life Architect. And my coaching combines cognitive psychology, clinical hypnotherapy, and a spiritual modality, which is unusual, because most of my colleagues want to stay on one track, and they want you to fit your square peg into their round hole. I'm the reverse. I would rather you just figure it out for yourself. I will provide you with all the tools that I'm currently aware of, and together we will figure you/it out, together.

Just remember, this is about coaching, guiding, and leading. We are going to do this together, and everyone I have ever coached, from athletes all the way to CEO's or private companies, we do it together. I am going to tell you right up front: I am just messed up as you are; I'm just aware that I am. That's the only difference. Let's get this real clear: I don't walk around with an air of piety just because I have some degree. Beyond that is learning and in my case, at least in part, unlearning someone else's information and giving it back to them for a grade and "degree."

Get ready for five steps: There are some theories that suggest that knowledge means nothing without application. Do not get caught up in that. I am going to ask you for the next five steps and during your reading of this book to suspend everything you think you know about the anatomy of your brain; how the actual functioning of your nervous system with your sympathetic system inside and out creates the manifestation of material items or experiences. Some of you may have read a fun little book that came out a while ago. It was about ten years or so ago, called "The Secret," which by the way is not a secret, and is also not how it really works, but it was a great marketing tool. It did make everybody believe that it indeed was a secret. How do they know what I don't? How did that happen? I will show you how it really works step-by-step.

So, lets agree on the following: Life is up and down like a wave in the ocean; it's topsy-turvy, right? Yet, most of us tend to approach it this way: "Everything is where I want it, so don't change. I just want everything to stay the same." Remember that I said that. Here is the first one that I am going to ask you to agree to: **Everything is**

a thought/feeling before it's internal or external reality. Meditate on that for a second and really think about it. By the way, this is fun, because you had to think about thinking about it, didn't you? Everything is going to boil down to thought. Simply put—an unfortunate little bit of carnage in this example—but if I lop off your head, the problems you face are immediately solved. Wouldn't you agree?

Next journey: There will be no more problems, no more neurosis, no more worrying about weight, and no more worrying about money. It is over, *done*. Follow me? I know it's a little morbid, but it drives the point home.

So, everything is going to be a thought/feeling before it becomes an internal/external reality. That is the first one. Next, **everything from the neck down is controlled from the neck up**. Again, if I lop off your head, your body doesn't do a whole lot. It will twitch for a couple of seconds, I'll give you that, but then it's over. So, therefore, everything from the neck down is on an auto-pilot sequence based on what the mind is telling it to do. Things do not happen randomly. It's just so habitual for me to shake my hand at an unconscious level that I do not have to think about it anymore, but I am thinking about. I'm just not aware that I'm thinking about it. Are you with me? Excellent

The Reality: The third thing is, wait for it… *Reality*! This one is going to stretch your boundaries a little. **There is no such thing as "reality," only the perception of reality**. Want to chew on that one for a second? That might make some smoke come out of your ears, I understand. There is no such thing as reality. If that were true, both of us right now would be experiencing this the same way, which is not happening. It is only perception. It stands to reason that if we alter someone's perception, we alter their reality both internally and externally. If you've ever had too much alcohol, you've altered your perception. You might not want to do it again, but you've done it.

The Four Corner Explanation: So that we can extrapolate what it means by "there is no such thing as reality and that only perception exists," imagine there's an intersection and you have four corners with one person standing on each corner. Two cars come together and BAM! They collide. As you'd expect, they call the police to take a report. The officer shows up and takes a report from each of the four people standing on each corner. Now, how many reports is this officer going to get? Six, if you count the two people in the car, but four is correct. Why? *Different perceptions.* Is it possible? Standing on the street corner looking from a point of view, one only sees that part of the picture. It doesn't mean that the other three points of view are not present, one is just not aware of them because one can only see from their point of view. Therefore, that becomes their reality; that point of view. Does it mean it is the right one? Yes, it's right for that point of view, but does it mean it is the total omnipotent right one? No. This is where we start to get communication breakdown.

The problem is: It's too good to be true; it's too simple. Everything in our world is complex, or more specifically, we make it complex. This is so simple; it's too easy. So, from their point of view it becomes difficult to see the other three corners. We are all guilty of that. If I am standing on the street corner right here and another is on the opposite corner looking from their point of view, they would see it totally differently. You say, "What is wrong with you? What, are you blind? What is the matter with you?" This happens when presenting a business plan. "Don't you see what I see? No." We get frustrated, don't we?

The Four Corner Explanation is a great way to explain to somebody, "I understand that you may know this point of view, but *is it possible* that there are other points of view for you to explore." What are they going to say then? They have to say, "Yes." It is called a "psyche" bind. It is a psychological structured set up. It is called a "bind," because they have to acknowledge that there are other points of view. Therefore, if there are other points of view, they have to step outside of what they just objected to. Does that make sense? The moment that they side-step, guess what happens? Their mind opens up. Hey, that was easy. Instead of fighting them head to head, just invite them like this and bind them. "How about we see it from this point of view?" "Oh, okay." That's what coaching is, isn't it? It's just getting them to see other options. That is all. *Therefore, we can change our external realities by changing our internal perceptions.*

Example: If I were to hypnotize a group via general hypnosis and say, "Look deep into my eyes," (Which, by the way, has nothing to do with the truth. We will use that for fun, because that is a stereotypical perception, right?) We all would think to ourselves, "Do not look in his eyes because he is going to hypnotize me." But hypnosis has nothing to do with my eyes or any swinging watches or anything like that. It has to do with actually developing the brain wave called "*theta wave.*" It's the use of words to communicate a state of mind. If I alter your perception and say, "Guess what? The wall nearest to you as you read this, when I count from one to three, is now green," you will see it from that point of view, even though the rest of us, who are "awake" near you, see it as beige or brown or whatever. Would you agree? Which one of us is right? We both are, because our perception is the only thing that is in question, and you cannot question perception because it is an internal experience. Does that make sense? Therefore, you are not wrong. I am not wrong. You are not right. I am not right. It just is. That is just how I see it. Cool, I see how you see it. Let me just switch around like this and invite you to see another point of view. If you like it, let's roll. If not, you can at least see their point of view and side-step their objections and stop battling. Does that make sense?

They all are hypnotized

It's a process of capturing the entire attention of a person, and that leads to too much time spent battling one another. I've seen it often. I've traveled around the globe and heard people say, "Hmm, we are making this way too hard," but it's because we are trying to get others to see our point of view. The catch is that they can't because we are all already self-hypnotized. Part of what the *"Finding out who you are not project"* has been doing is the opposite of what we've known for the last twenty-one years. It's to say, "You know what? We're not here to hypnotize you. We're here to use hypnosis just to *wake you up*." Be honest with yourselves you get up and drink your coffee the same way you always do. You brush your teeth the same way. You say, "Would you like to see my _____ Business Plan?" "I have been talking to everybody. They are just not getting it." You get frustrated, right? That's because you're fighting both yours and their perception. That doesn't make much sense, now does it? So, instead, you're all going to break your own perceptions.

We can change our realities because the truth is: the person you were when you started reading this book and the person who you'll be by the time you've finished it will be completely different, because you cannot unlearn what you're learning here. I'm altering your perceptions as we read, and you're doing it with me. Change has to occur from each of us, individually, from the inside in order for the "outside" world(s) to evolve.

Change inside you: Once you change your perception, people are going to notice something different about you. My goal for you over the next five evolutions is that you finally find peace with yourself, because all human beings are capable of doing so. How you chose to do it is up to you. I am going to offer you a wide berth to do it over the pages that follow, but that's what we're looking for, isn't it?

You've heard the story over and over again: Someone works their butt off for 40 hours a week and finally finds success. But at what cost? They're married, but to their work. Whether it's a job, a business we own, so on and so forth, the mindset is: "I don't want to lose all I've worked for." Isn't that an interesting mindset? We will get back to that later.

Remember, we can change our external realities by changing our inside. Everything is a thought inside before it becomes outside. This holds true for every human being, every one of us. It's common ground. Don't believe me? Test it. Play around with it.

Therefore, what changes our perceptions is our *beliefs*. You're going to *change your beliefs*. Now, I'm not going to do that for you, because who am I to tell you what to believe? That's a God complex and anyone who's ever met me can tell you, I'm no God. That's not to say I'm a bad guy by any means, but, well... you get the point.

So anyway, we change our own beliefs, and it does not happen from outside in, but rather from inside out. For example, if we believe this "business" is hard; guess what the person on the other side looking back at you is going to pick up on? They are just going to saying, "I don't get it." It's unconscious. Your projection is part of the problem. I know that doesn't feel good to read, but it's the truth. They're picking up on your "inner reality" and it's making *their* reality that much more difficult. Another inner-belief example I hear from some of my business clients is, "Well, if you're not successful, how am I going to be successful? You're the one who took the jump and it hasn't worked out for you so far. So, I'm going to stay over here where I don't have to jump, and I'm going to watch you fall. It's much more entertaining." Does that make sense? Have you heard this before or even said to yourself? Sure you have. Does anybody disagree with what you believe is true for you? No one is right, and no one is wrong. It's just what they believe.

Internet peoples: People on the Internet, this is not that hard. It took me two degrees to figure it out, but I promise you, after these chapters, you will figure it out in about twenty minutes. What I couldn't figure out was: How do I figure out a system to help people figure their "internal" self out? That is why we're here to share knowledge; we're all in the "people business" in some way or another. Can anybody really deny that? This is the part that I saw from my point of view, and I'm interested to see from yours. Are you experiencing some of these things out there? My suspicion is that you are, especially in today's world where everything is about fear. Fear is a great irony. If you look at history, whenever there has been an economic downturn and fear has been the preponderance that has been when most of the great fortunes have been made. So, when one point of view says, "The sky is falling," the other point of view says, "Huh, the sky is mine-I'm buying it dirt cheap, and I'm just going to wait." You guys have to decide what part of the fence you are on. What you believe is true. These are the things that I am going to ask you to believe now.

This is your first homework assignment   It is a very specific question:

What are three beliefs you need to achieve the reality that you desire?

1._____

_____

2._____

_____

3._____

_____

First of all, that's also going to predicate something else. What *is* your desire? Most folks say, "I just want to be rich." What the does that really mean? I don't have a clue what that means to you. Do you know yourself? It's just a word and we have to know what it is we REALLY want. The problem is that most of us honestly don't know.

Ultimately, the unfortunate truth is when you're faced with, "Hey, you can have anything you want," you stand there and say, "I have no clue what I want." If you have not had that experience, you have not reached what you want yet, because the first time I had it, I was surprised. I consider myself a pretty educated man and I walked in and said, "I can have anything I want. What the heck do I want?" I sat in what is called a "conscious lock." You will learn about that in a minute. I was just dumbfounded. I had no idea what I wanted. Now, imagine the person who hasn't even had the opportunity to explore what they want at all. They are in "survival" mode, which is what most of the people that you probably engage daily with are in. Probably even yourself. When you're in survival mode, these questions scare the daylights out of you because they're too big. The funny thing is: It's exactly where we need to be. It starts right here. It does not start with saying, "Hey, guess what? I am going out and ….." Most of my experience so far is that people go out with a big, big bang, kind of peak fast, and it just kind of fizzles. It's kind of like a helium balloon. Have you had that experience yet? I'm willing to bet you have.

Sidebar: No one sat in the reserved seat. (Taken from a LIVE workshop) Why is that? Why didn't anybody sit there? Why is it reserved? I didn't put the sign there. I just said it was reserved. I didn't say you couldn't sit there. Isn't it interesting how we create *"limiting beliefs"* which create rules? I did not create the rules. I just put the sign there to see who would sit there and say, "You know what? Screw that. I'm going to sit there. It is reserved for me!" I wanted to see who would have the guts to break the "rules," because the rules are what are keeping you, your entire organization, and everybody you come upon in their "box." The entire essence of this book is for you to get the concept that there is no box. It's an illusion exacerbated by the fact that your mind controls your body, and your body is forced to comply. You may have heard the old saying, "The road to hell is paved with great intentions." Intentions are just a spark, but the engine has got to turn over, and that's what the other three points of view are about. Okay. You do not have to do this right now, but start pondering. What three beliefs are needed right now? You have to ask yourself, "What beliefs do I have right now that are keeping me in my box?" That is going to make you stay up at night, and it should. The work that you're doing here will come back, tenfold or hundredfold or more if you choose.

Now the question we want to address is a very simple one, and yet it perplexes most people that I work with. It is one that I ask all the time. "**Are you ready?**" Most will say, "Well, I'm ready now." If you are not ready, don't worry; you're not a bad person. In fact, it might mean that you're a smart person because you're stopping long enough to admit that you're not ready, and to think about why that is. Ultimately, that's the truth of what's really going on inside. Example: "I am not going to go out unprepared and make a total fool of myself and turn this business opportunity into another unfulfilled idea that could have worked if only I hadn't gotten in my own way." Does that sound familiar? It doesn't feel great, I know.

You have got to have the real "*inner psychological power*" to get through the internal changes you want to make. Otherwise, you're just over there saying, "Yeah, I feel great!" Then, you go out and the world slaps you right in the face. So you freeze, and now the next time you think about going out and giving the world another shot, you hesitate. If it happens often enough, you might choose to never try it again. Not only are you aware that "belief" came from your original internal box, but you've now added another one that sounds something like, "People are scary. This/that is scary," which is totally not true. When you get over the fear, you begin to understand what's really happening, that everyone is just as "messed up" as you and haven't figured it out yet either. If you stay in that box, you'll never be able to make progress and achieve the life you deserve. You need to be willing to break the rules, even if you end up flat busted and broke, which, by the way, is basically a necessary part of life. History mandates virtually all the great ones have busted out at least three times in bankruptcy before they became billionaires. That means you only have two more times and presto!

Get excited: All right, let's get you down to some anatomies so you understand some things more deeply. What I am about to show you, people, I promise you have not learned. You probably have not heard this before. When you walk away with this at the end of the chapter, you will be able to mess with yourself in a whole new, fun way, and I mean that. Look, its all psych-warfare, whether you're psyching yourself out or you're dealing with somebody else. That's the bottom line. More often than not, it's working with you. This is the anatomy. Let's make this simple; I do not want to get into a big, long debate about the multiple sides of the brain. How about we just have two brains, conscious and unconscious/subconscious? You choose whichever word you want. Simple. I want you to look at the conscious mind as "The Guard." Imagine in your mind right now, that there is a beautiful castle, and standing outside of this castle, by the drawbridge, is a single guard with a spear. His job is to make sure that whoever goes in and out of that gate is, of course, cleared by the "conscious mind." Now, the funny thing about the conscious mind is it seems to forget that there are three other walls that are not being guarded at that castle and there's a whole lot of other activity he's not aware of; and, because of certain things that I am going to show you right now, he convinces you[1], that everything is under control, which, by the way, is also an illusion.

---

[1] I used "he." It could be a "she" depending on the type character voice you assign in your head. You get my point.

CHAPTER # 2

Mental process and its Control

(Activity, Thinking, Feeling and Remembering)

How much do you really control? The answer, dear reader, is one thing. That's it; you get one thing that you get to control outright in this Universe. Everything else is a probability based on "extrapolation of human beings being on the planet for about, oh, I don't know, 200,000 years. The rest of it is a guess. It is hopeful. Hope is tricky because it has variables of, "No," meaning N-O versus K-N-O-W. Let's move on to the *"Guard of the Gate."*

Do you know what that one thing is? Let's take a guess, what is the one thing that you control? Your thoughts? Well how about this: Don't think of the color red right now. You just did. Now who controlled that, you or me? I did because of the rules of the conscious mind, that's the only reason. So, you don't control your thoughts specifically. If that were true, you would right now be paying attention the entire time I have been explaining this concept, during this reading, and you have not. Now, not all comes from the subconscious; a lot does but not all. That's another illusion. So, what is the one thing you control? Interestingly, even the Spirit has one rule that "you" control. What is it, you ask? It happens as a process and it starts with a "D" - Decide or Decision. Simply put you control "choice." You can decide one way, or you can decide another - You control the choice. **You** control who you talk to, you control how you choose to respond (most often, except when in reaction mode), you control how you feel; you control most everything about choice. Spirit will give you the opportunity, which is what a "MOG" is. This book is a MOG (Moment of Grace). It's the calling of your spirit saying, "Hey, wake up! There's an interesting choice here, and if you choose it, there's a whole other avenue that you haven't even thought of yet."

Otherwise, there wouldn't be that last book in the Bible that starts with an "R." If everybody were nice and didn't have individual choice, they wouldn't have had to write that book in the first place. Here is another example: How many times have you had fun with this one, commonly called the New Year's resolution? "I am going to work on my willpower. I am going to change some habits this year. My New Year's Resolution is to change some habits. I am going change this or that habit. I am going to change my habit of habits. That's what I am going to change." How is your willpower these days? Did you know that Will-Power is a conjunction of two words, which is why it is hyphenated here, "will" and "power." **Willing to have power but does not**. That is why it fails all the time. That's why when you go and you make that New Year's Resolution to go to the gym, the gym hopes you fail. They know that after about seven days your conscious willpower will probably stop working because it doesn't have the strength left to keep up the new habit. The illusion is that it does, because of other beliefs like "I am a very educated person; I'm in control of myself; I decide everything (except for going to the gym) but I will pay for it for the next three years so I can feel better about myself because I had the *intention* of getting in great shape." How many times have you gone through this process?

Gyms have built entire business models on this little known fact. It's a great psychological battle. It works perfectly and we keep repeating the process year after year. The special promotion this year is $36 bucks and I am going to use you this time. I am going to be in this gym 7 days a week! Then you start your new journey and about three days in, you find out that lactic acid burns, it hurts. Or, "Oh, God I didn't even know I had that muscle. Where did that come from?" This is the **psychological pain/pleasure pendulum**. You will move away from pain and towards pleasure, even though the money is where the pain is.

Random thoughts

The next step is the conscious mind (the guard of the castle). It holds only one thought per second. One thought per second, which is when we stop and notice our "thoughts," and we can see that they are so random. See, you just had another one; right here reading and again you are not controlling it. It's like someone put a gremlin in your head, and it makes up stuff. I mean, since you have been sitting here, you have thought about "stuff" that has nothing to do with this book, why you are reading it, or even yourself. You have gone wondering off about "stuff" you haven't even thought about yet, and you're saying, "Where did that come from?" You will go think about it for a while until you wander off into something else. It's kind of like the lost leading the lost. So, when you're doing a presentation, going on a first date, or whatever, this is part of what you're dealing with both inside you, and with those you're interacting with as well.

The Conscious Mind only holds seven pieces of information at one time, give or take, plus or minus two items, depending on the person's memory ability, before it locks up. A dog, when you make a strange noise, it turns its head sideways and thinks "huh" well human beings do that too. Have you ever had six or seven people talk to you at the same time and you can't handle it. That's why; the Guard cannot handle that much information. So, when you're bombarding someone with information regardless of the situation, it overwhelms him or her. Their natural reaction is to close the "drawbridge" of their mind and get you out of their headspace. They don't even know why. Psychologically, we're all built that way.

In today's world, it is **statistically estimated** that we will get presented with roughly 3,000 advertisements per day: Internet, television, radio, billboards, by our friends, etc. If we didn't have some filtering process, we would be robots. I have an example of a beer company that had a great advertising campaign; they had the frogs and the iguanas. Can you guess what brand I'm speaking of? Of course, it's Budweiser, and you know that through a process called programming through bombardment, which occurs during the advertisement.

The stuff that you are learning here in this chapter will change you because you are going to watch people walk around in a fog. When you do, have some fun with them: walk up to them and ask, "What is the name of that dog from the fast food commercial? I can't remember the name of it." They will say, "Chihuahua." You say, "I was talking to somebody the other day, and I was trying to remember what it was associated with," and of course they'll tell you that it was Taco Bell. The object is to get them out of their mind as they are in it, as we are, until we are aware of it. That is the first freedom that we must seek to get out of our heads, because it has rules. Rules that are easily broken.

Toast your noodle: *The Conscious Mind is linear in relationship to time.* If you notice the randomness of your thoughts, the one thought per second, it is usually about a *future event,* which is in one-second increments, and thus it keeps moving. Therefore, it keeps looking at this current moment as a past event or one that is coming up next. If you notice, you are never standing still. Hence the term: *stream of consciousness.* It just keeps going. It's like a stock ticker. That is why when you go to bed at night; your mind is thinking off all the things you have to do the next day. We are all this way, just in varying perceptual degrees. We go to bed thinking and we wake up thinking. We wonder why we're tired and exhausted. We're never still, at least on the inside. People who notice their stream of consciousness notice that it's a lot of noise. If you cannot interrupt the stream of consciousness, you're doomed to repeat what is going by on the "ticker" inside your head. Let's have some more fun: Have you ever met someone now and instantly liked them, but weren't sure why? We call that *synchronicity in our world.* Repeat that question back yourself without rereading it, as I said it above or with your best guess. Now, let's go one step further. I used your conscious mind's rules to elicit a truthful, subconscious response because the conscious mind is the only thing that lies, but I asked your subconscious to answer honestly. Forgive that I used a conscious rule with you; allow me extrapolate this for you. The "Now" question, the funny thing is… remember, I just said, (I gave you a hint a minute ago.), "hiding in the obvious" is how suggestion and passing the guard at the gate works. The question again is "Have you ever met someone **now** and instantly liked them, but weren't sure why?" Did you catch it that time? What word are you missing from the first reading? Why are you missing it at all? Simple, "now," to a conscious linear mind gets deleted from the sentence when it is repeated back because it does not make sense to the Guard because "Now" just left. It just left again, as a past event (that 1 second is gone). If you watch what I did, I gave what is called a *"physiological subconscious response,"* which is a real nice way of saying, "I just gave you a suggestion." I said, "Hey, have you ever met somebody *now*." (I am pointing towards the center of my chest when doing this at the LIVE workshops, reader). Have you ever met somebody *now*? I am pointing to myself, while asking this question and at the same time the word "now" comes out of my mouth.

When this is done the person sees my hands "subconsciously" point to myself, and "Have you ever met someone now and instantly liked them, but weren't sure why?" You are thinking at one thought per second; you did not "see" me slip that word *now* in there. Even though you heard it subconsciously, you did not hear it consciously. I told you the rule above being employed here. The **conscious linear mind** said, "Well, the word *now* does not make sense because now is then. It is the past." So, it deletes it from the sentence. Unconsciously, this is what happened to your mind, as you read it above this first time. You went back to somewhere in your memory, and you found someone that you liked, associated with now and kind of built up a rapport with this person in your head. Then like the old Chihuahua on the dashboard of your car with its head bobbing up and down while you drive, I continued to say, "That you met, and you liked, and you did not know why," and then, all of your heads starting nodding "yes." It is a physiological command to the subconscious, as by now your conscious guard is overloaded. It is fun at a party; because, if you drink, you're fair game. I will have you doing hand signals. You will look like a baseball coach. You will not even know why you are doing it. Suggestion is powerful.

The reason behind this phenomenon is three-fold. To a conscious linear mind, the word *now* does not make sense. Now, do I recommend that you start off this new journey and walk around asking people a "Now" question to people? You might be a little rough with it. Don't say, "Have you ever met somebody *now* (steep emphasis on NOW and the pointing to yourself) that when you met them right away you like them, and you did not know why?" They will dismiss you immediately, as the conscious guard goes into full alert. What makes it even more fun when I do this in my live show is that the word *now* is up there on screen when I ask the question. Do you see how easy it is for us to get locked up into our own stuff? It's easy to lock us up. This is what most people are doing all day, and they don't even realize it. Imagine how they are suffering. They are beyond self-hypnotized. They are programmed and reprogramming themselves at the same time. We were all guilty of that at one time or another.

The next rule of the conscious mind: Is called ***the Three D's of the Conscious Brain:***

1. Deletes.
2. Distorts.
3. Do's/Don't & Generalizes.

The reason we call it the "Three D's," is because it originally started out as three D's; but now the third is called *generalizing*. We changed it because we realized that we all make global assumptions. "All network marketing is a scam." *Pyramid*, is also a great word. People create a generalization off of a one-time experience and it becomes an all-encompassing "rule" in their mind. Here it is in a ***microcosmic version***: You are a young kid, sitting down, playing with the dog's food, and your parents say, "Hey, don't play with that because the dog is going to bite you." You know more than your parent does, as we all do at that age, and you stick around for a while, and to no one's surprise, the dog bites you. Now advance to the future, years later and you hear the sound, "Ruff!" and immediately you're reminded of the dog's bite all those years ago. From that moment on, and for the rest of the life, every time you approach a dog, you approach it cautiously. You think, "Wait a minute, ALL dogs bite."

You have created a generalization that all dogs bite. It's not true, but you made it true to yourself. Therefore, it is true. "All network marketing is pyramid schemes." If that were true, nobody would be making any money with them. *Somebody* is making money. After all, Amway has been around a long time. The problem is: They only work for people who are awake enough to see it, or at least willing to be awake. Maybe you're doing the same. If someone throws a big fishnet out, he's going to catch a whole bunch of fish. But if he waits, and has a harpoon, maybe he'll land himself a nice, big, white whale.

CHAPTER 3

Architect360 Training

(Social Learning and Social Cognition)

What do I mean by brain wave power? We are more than one brain wave, we are four different waves and all human beings operate via these four:

- Beta.
- Alpha.
- Theta.
- Delta.

Beta is what you are now as you are reading this, consciously aware, meaning cognitively awake. At some point most readers will slip into *Alpha*, which is kind of like a daydream. You are in kind of a trace-like state while reading. *Delta*, what you normally sleep in, is slow-wave sleep, REM state[2]. The third one is called *Theta,* and Theta waves are where you relax and sleep well. You know that Sunday afternoon nap on the couch, and for some strange reason, 20 minutes feels a whole lot better than 8 hours? That's because you're

---

[2] Rapid eye movement sleep (REM sleep, Slow Wave Sleep cycles) is a unique phase of mammalian sleep characterized by random movement of the eye

in a Theta wave state, which is an ideal place to be for rest. The mind and body are harmonizing and synchronizing.

So let's talk about it: Now, we are in our full consciousness at Beta. The APA, the American Psychological Association, says we can use anywhere from 2% to 10% of our brain at any given moment. That means right now you are using, maybe, 2% to 9%, if you are lucky. Let's call it two for a simple number. Of that 2%, 10% is what your conscious brainpower represents, and you wonder why willpower fails; it doesn't have any power. It is an illusionary power; its job is to defend. That brings us to the next rule of the conscious mind: ***Creates value judgment***. It's the only part of us that creates value judgment, but it creates it based off distorted, deleted, and generalized concepts. So, what if we could change our belief structure and thereby change how we value things. Wouldn't that be an interesting, powerful thing to use when you are talking to people who do not understand value yet?

- The value of an idea.
- The value of a concept.
- The value of a marketing concept. (Example: Corporate American Business model versus Network Marketing Business model– value judgment created the difference here)

They call it corporate America and just changed the perception of what a business model should look like. It sounds cool, because there is a president, a million or so vice presidents, a whole bunch of junior vice presidents, and senior managers. The base gets wider and wider as you get lower and lower; hence, the term "pyramid." They've been doing this for years, but it's socially acceptable. If one does it for themselves, then it's a pyramid scheme and yet it's the same concept when viewed without the "value judgment" concept from our minds. The funny thing is, at the end of the corporate ladder, they kick you out and give you a gold watch and say, "Good luck." By the way, you do not even get COBRA for health care for very long." It's simply a gold-plated watch and "Psych!" They kick you out, and you have no say in the matter. No choice. Mandatory retirement — you're outta here. If we decided that we're doing it for ourselves, people call it "risky" or "foolish," because you might fail. At least you can't get fired, reach an earning ceiling, or get a fake, gold-plated watch – unless you buy it for yourself, In which case it will have more value to you since you chose to buy it!

Randomness in nature

Randomness in nature means our thoughts are random. They just come through the stream of consciousness randomly. It has so much stuff inside, and it even makes "stuff" up sometimes. It is entertaining to "watch" from inside... at least some times. The next rule of the conscious mind is that *it's negative or pessimistic by nature*. Its job is to keep things out of your brain that might make you change, those patterns inside your subconscious mind. So by design, it is negative and/or pessimistic by its "*nature*." It doesn't mean that you're a negative person or you're pessimistic, it means your conscious mind will approach most things from that point of view, regardless of what comes out of your mouth. Haven't you noticed whenever you hear that someone else maybe got a promotion, or they got an executive suite faster than you; Isn't it your first reaction to say something like, "Who do they know to get that?" We take it personally. We make it personal so we can say that it's negative or pessimistic by nature. When you are approaching somebody new for the first time that's what you are battling. It is not the person. It's that defense mechanism. So, just side step it, just go right around it, and stop arguing with it. Meanwhile, you're arguing with the same thing because you've got one too. So, it's two negative or pessimistic things arguing against each other, and we all know that two negatives do not make a positive. That's another illusion. What ends up happening is polarizing. The person says,

"You are a _____. I don't want to be anywhere near you. You're like a virus; you must be tainted." Then, embarrassed, you turn red, and they can't be around you anymore. Maybe you tried to "sell" them something that they didn't want, which by the way, totally negates their ability to make a choice. But that's what they do; it's what we all do.

"*Don't*" and "*try*." These are two words, earlier when I said "Don't think of the color red." Most readers thought of the color red in some form or another. The word "don't" to the conscious mind is deleted; and, everything after the word "don't" is what actually happens. We heard, "*Touch the stove,*" versus "*Don't touch the stove,*" because a conscious mind deletes the word "don't." So, when you're out there talking with people, and you hear the word "don't" or you say the word "don't," everything after that is what is going to happen. Maybe we say, "Now, don't look at this as network marketing. Look at it as a people business. Don't look at it as network marketing." The first thing they hear is, "It *is* network marketing. It's a scam and a type of pyramid or something.

I am going to challenge you from now on, decide to eliminate the word "don't" from your vocabulary and become consciously aware of how often other people around you use it. As soon as they say it, call them on it, and watch how they change.

Now, the word "*try.*" This is one of the worst communication words in both personal and professional engagements. A lot of people say this, "Just give it a try. It will happen all by itself." This is what happens when we "try." I am not going to move. I want you readers to imagine a pencil or pen in my extended hand and to "try" to take the pen from me. I said, "try" to, and not touching it is not doing it. Now "try" to. Actually there is no "try." (Hey, turns out Yoda was right!) It's an illusion. There is no such thing as "try." The point here is to **get honest** and **be honest** with you. Because if you can't try, you can't try with the person you are talking to. There is no "try," but we are taught in the English language to, "Give it a try." Do you remember what happened when you tried in athletics? They said,

"Get up there and just try to hit the ball." It's moving at 80 miles per hour! In golf, you try to hit a tiny little ball 200 yards, through all that wind and whatnot. "Just try and put it over there." The question here is how you can try, well! You have to swing the club and hit the ball, not try to, period. If someone doesn't break down the technique and teach you how to do it, you'll look like Charles Barkley trying to swing a club out there. No one wants that. See, that's the power of conscious contact, though the art of language. We are not "trying" to show someone how to do or be _____. We are *showing* them _____, otherwise, you're doomed to go around and around in circles, and "don't" get mad when they tune out. It's our fault. We are responsible. "Don't" and "Try." Those two little words are like bonuses that allow us to change almost instantly, just by being aware of them in others and ourselves.

I challenge you to "try" it for one week, and be honest with yourself so you can see how quickly you revert to your old habits. Hopefully, you'll be aware enough that you won't. You may trip and fall along the way, but you are becoming awake. What happens when you first go back to the gym? Your muscles wake up. Like your muscles, your brain has been asleep for a long time, and it's just another organ in your body. I promise you that when you meet eternity, your brain will not be going with you. Your mind will, but not your brain. It's going right back to the dirt. The brain itself is just a tool. It has a job to do just like your liver, your stomach, and everything else.

Let's have some fun. This is where it all really happens, the subconscious mind and the ***"King of the castle."*** Recall there are three points of view in the intersection example. We're just not aware of them. Isn't it nice to know that we have a brain that runs our heartbeat for us? If we had to do it consciously, we'd all be dead. The amount of brainpower it takes just to make the heart go, "bump-bump" one time would just overwhelm us. In fact, I can tell you psychologically and anatomically that it is accomplished by a series of synapses firing signals in our neural network that goes to our *nervous system* and *sympathetic nervous system,* which make my muscles contract and expand. Which is a nice way of saying, thank God my subconscious brain is in control, because I have no clue. If you told me that I had to make my finger contract consciously, I could not tell you what muscles make it work or how to tell them to work together. I just couldn't do it. It wouldn't happen.

This is the interesting part: There are no rules for the Subconscious, as it houses the *imagination.* Imagination only has one rule; everything is thought before it comes out into the external world. Some architect, somewhere on this wonderful planet, thought of a beautiful house, and it exists now because they built it. If you, dear reader, had an idea when someone came to you and said, "I want you to take a look at this concept." It is still just a concept at this point. It was something you may have seen on the web. It may be something you had had a conversation about. Someone showed you an opportunity, and you went, "Aha! I know people who would get this." You didn't get it, you just imagined that you got it, but it became real instantaneously. It became so real inside, you made a decision.

Subconscious and Imagination:

Your imagination holds thousands of thoughts per second, every day and all day. It may not be exactly thousands; actually it's probably closer to almost millions at this point. It extrapolates data so fast that we cannot even really comprehend how much it really handles. The neuron matrix in our brain is so complex we can't even map it. It just goes off in nanoseconds. A nanosecond is one billionth of a second. There are thousands and thousands of thoughts, most we are not really consciously aware of, and that is a double-edged sword.

It never "locks up," ever; because if it does, game over. It will constantly work for you because it is a wonderful thing called a *servomechanism*, or solution-oriented mechanism. Its job is to solve problems. That's it. The imagination is where it all comes from. Later, we will prove that it's ALL only imagination, "Well, I can imagine it this way, and this is what I can do with it." You brought your imagination to the table, and that is called the collective. Next rule:

Three dimensional in relation to time, means:

- The past.
- This current moment.
- Your potential life – commonly called the future.

They are all one. They are all the same simultaneously. Therefore, let's suppose someone has a phobia about dogs like we discussed earlier; we can go back into their imagination via the subconscious mind, reshape the perception of how one "sees" that dog experience and it instantaneously ripples through that entire timeline to all their potential unrealized futures, and suddenly it's as real as the original experience itself. That is the *power of the subconscious mind*. I have been doing it for 25 years and some people want to call it *hypnosis*. Some people want to call it NLP; some people want to call it Ericksonian Therapy. Some people want to call it good old fashioned brainwashing, which by the way is not true because if this were brainwashing, I would have much bigger results with people worldwide. It is three-dimensional, which means you can make a future event feel real right now. What ends up happening is through what's known as "*manifesting.*" You've undoubtedly heard this term; it's a very popular psych term now, but what it means is energy draws to like energy. If a thought is energy, when you put so much energy into a future perceptional value, an idea, you're naturally drawn to it. These weird "coincidences" start showing up via people, signs/

messages, and experiences. Your conscious mind jumps in says, "It cannot be that simple." If you're not paying attention, you will say to yourself, "You're right" and go back to trying to figure out what's wrong. The funny thing is, nothing is wrong. You are just making it wrong. It was always right. You put your energy where you wanted it to go, and your subconscious was responding. It was drawing what you wanted to you, because when you first got your new "idea" and became excited and everybody was coming out of the woodwork to support that. So you imagine ways to grow it and expand it, it's all roses, until you run into a belief that may not be inline and your conscious mind jumps all over you with negative thoughts and doubts. If you do not reel those in and address your beliefs and change their perceptions, the idea fizzles out and goes away as your thought energy gets smaller and smaller. Not unlike any other muscle, you must use and pay attention to it or it will deteriorate and eventually fade into the abyss of unrealized potentials.

What we do: Know this and applying it helps us create what I call an *"Auto code."* The stream of consciousness is always going to be with you as long as you are in this human body. It is part of the ego attached to the conscious mind. It's an inevitable part of the anatomy. You can interject in the consciousness, but you want to do via this imagination thing over here in your subconscious. Now, we are going to start an experience on how to do that. If you put it right into your auto coding, it will naturally draw it right to you. You don't have to do anything. In fact, when you do "something," you will mess it up. It will seem too easy if you just stepped back and think nothing is happening. It is like us going over there and telling that palm tree how to grow. If you want a great tree, let it grow, stop bothering it. This is a whole new concept. You probably haven't heard this stated this way, but I see it from a completely different point of view. I am not saying it is the "right" one, but I think it's got merit. The subconscious holds no judgment; it's a computer, people. Just a computer. It runs on a series of programs or auto-codes and it does not make value judgments, it just solves problems. It doesn't care whether it's wrong or right because wrong or right concepts are consciously driven. It doesn't know. It just goes, if you start putting value judgments on it, that's you consciously intervening; and more often than not, most times it's your ego or a control factor. It runs programs. It's not random. It repeats the same thing every day. It's rather boring and monotonous, but at least it's dependable. People object to you or your ideas because of that fact right here, it is not a random objection; it is a program within their subconscious coupled by the value judgment of their consciousness. If you change their perception, you change their program, you don't change the external for them to agree, you change their internal perception to allow them to agree with whatever it is you're presenting, up to and including yourself as a person. It is not *brainwashing*. You are just slipping around their defense mechanism saying, "Let's just for one second see it from this point of view?" The moment they see it, their inner program that says, "I am with you," stops running the interruption program and another pathway is opened to create together. It is much more entertaining, and people become very entertaining to you.

Every person who has developed a strong business or any business has had the same challenge. "Where do I start getting competent people around me then grow it to where I can take a step back?" This is what marketing is, but we don't want to call it that. We want to call it a "scheme." It is a very simple presentation. I decide when I go to work. I decide what my value is and whom I want to talk to. I decide when and where I'm going to do whatever I want to do, even if it means doing nothing. But that's a choice too, isn't it? Now, I'm responsible for my life, and that's a freedom very few people in our wonderfully free country have never experienced and that, to me, is *tragic*.

Moments of peace

This is the truth: All change comes from within. It's very simple stuff. For there to be long-lasting change, there must be an *auto-coded* program that changes the subconscious level inside out. It is not an outside-in sequence because it has to go through your conscious filters. If it goes through your conscious filter, it changes what it was, based on what it thinks it sees versus what you see unfiltered. Even though it may be a computer, we all will see different things due to our individual filtering. All of us are right, and all of us are wrong at the same time. If it is connected to spirit, it can't be wrong. People are from different deity structures: Christian, Muslim, Hindu and Jewish etc. That is your choice, but it still cannot be wrong because all of you at one time in your life had that moment where everything just lined up, and it felt right, and you had that moment of peace. It was a moment that everyone wants to get. No, you were not thinking that day. You let your natural spirit show up, and let yourself be you. Maybe all things are messed up externally, but still you were peaceful internally. Spirit showed up. You made the decision to get out of your way for once, and the next day "it" was seemingly gone. There are a series of levels, called the *"frustration levels."* You get to the point where you cannot take anymore. Then all of a sudden peace shows back up again. I wonder why that is? Maybe it is because you decided to get out of your way. That's a very frustrating way to do it, but it *is* a way. It's not the way I would recommend, but it's still a way. That is "**food for thought**."

From this moment forth, for the next five evolutions outlined here within this book, (after reading this you can go back to being as you want, that is your choice) we made an agreement on the things we are going to suspend about *reality*, how we choose to think, what the defense mechanisms are that we're dealing with, conscious and subconscious mind, and more that you are going to learn in the next chapters. Here is another: *Thoughts are things*. You can no longer afford the luxury of letting your mind run amuck, because if you do,

I promise you this: You will repeat the patterns of your past because you have not changed them from the inside out. Thoughts are real things. They are electrical synapses firing. It is an electrical charge. We can document that. It is called a "**synapses fire**." You can look it up yourself. Thoughts are Things, which brings us to a couple of philosophies that we are going to instill in you right now. Thought begins everything. We already agreed that thoughts are where it starts. It dovetails with this: Mental attitude creates everything we live and experience. Now, I am not talking about learned optimism via, Norman Vincent Peale, I understand his concept, but the truth is my conscious mind doesn't want to be positive. It will find a way to say, "This is _____," even when I do not want it to, and sometimes it's random, which is scary because I don't know what is going to happen. It might happen when I don't want it to.

Our thoughts and our fortune

Thought begins everything: These tend to flow one to the next: Before understanding, we must first recognize the infinite wisdom, power, and supply from within. These are very strong words to lock onto: Supply from within. Is there really a lack of abundance, perhaps it's because we haven't truly allowed it into our lives? That is the truth. It does not feel good, but we have to deal with it, or continue not having it. Look around you at this beautiful place you are at today called Earth. We are all part of it and we all go out and affect other people by sharing and being ourselves. What is inside us is not addicted to the external search for things. Jump to the *other side*: Harmony must begin on the inside before taking the form on the outside. When you go to do your "plan," your pitch, and you're all disheveled, all messed up, you just came off the phone, and you just can't get it together, you sit down and say, "Now, I want you to take a look at this calmly. I want you to understand something, because the truth is, we are doing business together. We do business together in any business that we are in. This one just happens to be _____, which, by the way, is a very simple business. It is so simple it kind of scares us. Wouldn't it be interesting if we sat down and said, "I want to do business with you, and I think you and me together could do some powerful things. Forget the business plan. Follow your dreams." This is a totally different approach.

No matter what business, it is a people business, but we rarely teach how to be in a people business in schools. So, we have an opportunity. We can choose from this moment forth, that our business is about people. Forget the business itself; the business part is a no-brainer. No pun intended. So, challenge yourself and completely put this aside. If you don't understand what you're talking about, how you're talking to the person, and what they want, how can you invite them and ignite their imagination? You'd be doomed from the start. "*Try* to look at this idea or _____ and what are they going to say." You'd be speaking a different language to them. Harmony with you: Be comfortable that you have chosen your business from the inside. Most of you are uncomfortable with what you are doing, as it is not fully "yours" yet. You are trying to make it happen. Let the palm tree grow. I know that scares you because you're used to being in control, but you were never in control anyway, remember? That was an illusion of the conscious mind.

Here is the deal: Consciousness creates results on the outside, from the inside. Be aware of what you are thinking, what you are doing, what choices you are making, and the words that come out of your mouth and the order and the sequence in which you put them. You have an awareness of yourself and if you don't, I believe you will by the end of this book. Everyone is random inside with respect to his or her thoughts and emotions. So it's the lost leading the lost, and you wonder why they don't see what you see. It's because we presented it in another way. If they ask you if you made a boatload of money at it, be honest. I have not made a lot of money at it, but I think that you and I can do it together. If I am doing my same old job, I know what I am going to make; That I do know, and I don't like it. I want more. Don't you? Notice how I used that positively.

Subconscious Mind - Link between brain and Spirit:

The first part is: The Subconscious is our link to our world within. It's our pathway, the bridge from our brain to our spirit. Our mind is the key, but not our brain. Our brain is just an organ. If there is no brain in the head, there is still the spirit. Start with spirit. That means your mind is still there. By the way, do we even know where the mind is? We cannot identify it and pinpoint the exact spot within the brain. It is somewhere. It is there. It's like the wind; we know it's there, but we have no idea where it starts or where it ends. We just know it's there. So we accept it. Accept that you have a brain and accept that you have a mind. If the brain is the hardware of our internal computer and our words are the ones and zeroes, then imagine the mind as the operating system. Here is an analogy to hopefully make it a little easier to process all this information. Every thought is a cause, and every condition is an effect. So, to take that further, the world within is the cause and the world without is the effect. Whatever is going on in here (mind/spirit), that is what you're going to see out here, whether you like it or not. These are God's rules. We never argue with God because he is bigger than us. The world within is the cause and the world without is the effect. If you do not have peace and calmness and a knowing that this is where you want to be, no one is going to join you for a long time. They will get caught up in the *zealousness.* No one said it was easy unless you make it easy. You were busting your butt before, and you may be doing it now. You're probably carrying a job and your dream at the same time, hopefully not, but it's not uncommon. If you are trying to do both, neither is being done to its fullest potential. "A double-minded man is unstable in all his ways." Not my words there.

Let's go to the **second part**. Most people build their *"pyramid of life"* in reverse. They start with the greatest margin, widest track, the biggest berth, and work up to the top. That is why they call network marketing a pyramid. They throw out the big net and some people rise to the top. That is the illusion. I disagree. It starts with the one who has the guts to go out and find the million others. It's a paradigm. That is how I approach my businesses. That is what I have done for 25 years. Look what I do for a living; I engage with people's heads. I'll be straight with you here, it is pretty entertaining.! I say, "I am going to "mess" with your head. You're not going to want to do it, and I'm going to have a whole lot of fun doing it." It is sadistic in a non-harmful light, but it's the truth.

I have seven billion potential clients. I get up every day and say, "Whom am I going to invite to change themselves today?" My friends know this about me, but they also know I love guiding people to live their dreams. We just did a round trip to New York, and the entire time, my assistant was saying, "Man, you never stop." There are people everywhere, and they are asleep via their own self-hypnosis. My job is to walk by and invite them to wake themselves up, which throws a thought in their mind. That it is possible to be something else, live a different life or way of life etc. Isn't it possible to believe in the impossible? The challenge is always available. If you are interested, then I have something I would like to show you. It is not the way. It is a way. It is a different invitation. First, nothing exists without the mind, barring spirit. If someone lops off your head, again the problem is solved. It is simple stuff. Secondly, recognition is the mental process of the internal world, and the fountain of supply and the external world is the outlet to the stream. It means when you recognize that you can go inside and that the spirit is within you, you call your Spirit (Allah, God, Yahweh or whatever). All your choice, whatever you call it, it is limitless only accept for what limits you place on yourself. Otherwise, all of this that you see would not be here. I have no idea how a palm tree grows. I have no idea of a magical moment where I take a seed that is about this big (size of acorn) and I throw it in the dirt, and there is some inevitable force that says, "Wake up seed." It pops open, and this huge beautiful tree comes out of nowhere. What are the odds that one right next to it looks like a palm tree, they look identical, but yet they are completely individual? How does that happen if they are both palm trees? These are the things I think about. You stare at a palm tree and think that it is some good stuff. You already are "fixed" in your spirit, but you are tossed up in your head just like everyone else. You can get out of your head, it is not inevitable that you stay there unless you choose to, which is your choice. Stop getting mad at everybody else when you choose it, or when the people around you choose it, let them choose it. Mess with it a little bit. Throw them some of these one-liners and watch their heads go, "blurb", and just leave them with it. Stop trying to ram a square peg down a round hole and expecting it to become flush; energy wasted. They will come around, maybe. If they do not, draw the people to you. Look for the millions based on your invitation. Not based on, "Well, you know what? You need to fit into what we are doing over here, and you have to fit in over here, and you need to do it this way." "I realize that you know how to run a business but this isn't that kind of business. You got to run it our way. That may be a dumber than dirt approach. We try to do it, because, "This is how we built the business." We listen to other people who have built their businesses. Maybe some of the other people in network marketing say, "Well, this is my business, and you should do what I did." "Well, that is really interesting except that there is only one of you. So, how can I be you?" That is impossible unless you can *step into their skin*, which they made a movie about called "Silence of The Lambs." I highly do not recommend that movie as a corporate training manual, by the way.

Homework

The first homework: An understanding of this process will give one abundance over poverty, wisdom over ignorance and peace over discord and more importantly, *Freedom* on all levels of existence. Freedom is what we all want: Financial, spiritual, emotional, physiological, sexual, psychosexual, relationship-oriented, self-relationship, God-oriented. We want freedom. We live in a country that is supposed to be based on freedom. Ironically we are less free than most people think we are. It is a strange irony, but it is true. We are a part of the problem. It is your business but get out of your mind. Free your mind and your fortune will follow. Write that one down, but I got the copyright on it.

Second homework: We do not just tell you how to and say, "Good luck." You experience it right here. If you cannot experience it here, I know you will not do it out there. You will give it a try and say, "I do not get it." You have probably had done this in your business, and someone else in your business has done it to you. In this methodology, when you are dealing with the mind, it is called: *Stillness.* Now, for some of you, that is going to "blow your brains out," because you have not sat still in a long time. I do not mean just sit still in the corner like "time out." I mean to sit still. I want you to select a place where you can be alone. Tonight, you are going to get few of your friends to join you and help you deal with it. I want you to sit as you are right now in a chair. Most of us try to lie in bed and clear our mind. "Oh, the alarm is going off in the morning. Yeah, I am good if I fall asleep." That is not what I am talking about. Get comfortable, but do not lounge. Let your thoughts roam where they will. They will because we already know the conscious mind is random. We already know the stream of consciousness is there; we do not have to participate in the stream of consciousness. You can choose to step back and say, "That is really interesting. Where did that thought come from?" Watch it go by like a movie. You have the best movie in your mind. You do not even have to pay for it; it's in your head. Watch how much "stuff" is in your head. It's amazing. It's almost overwhelming at first where you can go. Continue this for three to four days a week. Ideally, you will do this all the way until the next chapter. That is an ideal. It does not mean you have to. Don't get stuck in doing it. Come on guys, I am making this so obvious. I mean, it is like a Mack Truck. "Don't get stuck in doing this/get stuck in doing this," which means you will get stuck in doing it, get it?

I know you did not hear me say it because I said it and it went right by you. See how easy it is? When we teach the advanced stuff, assuming you go for it, we will teach you psychodynamics, where you can understand how it works from a physical breakdown. Some might find this extremely difficult. The reason you may find it difficult is because your conscious mind wants you to be out of control. It wants you to be out of peace. It wants you to be in "its" space. It wants you to feel uncomfortable because that is how it survives. It is necessary because then all of a sudden you have to use your logical deduction to work your way through stuff as opposed to just saying, "I am just going to go down here (Spirit) and *feel* my way through it." If we have already agreed that spirit is more intelligent, then why would you be relying on the conscious deductive power, which is what? 1% to 6%? I will take Spirits lead and take my chances.

So, some of you are going to find this easy. Some of you are going to go, "Thank God, I can have some peace." You might invite yourself to do it. I invite you to do that. Remember this: It is essentially to secure complete control of your body. This is not negotiable. Ignore your random thoughts and condition your body to be disciplined to what your brain tells it to do; because, if your body and your mind are disconnected, you will never have synchronicity. It is inevitable that you have to have synchronicity to find peace but you have to go down here (Spirit) to have it. Hopefully you get my point.

It is the ***foundation of everything*** we are going to do in the rest of this book; because, if we cannot make the decision and just sit still, everything else is lost in affording. That sounds tragic and it is a lot of pressure, but most of us were taught to keep going, move forward, strive, be successful, procreate, buy houses, buy cars, get successful, and get security, but I have never found security in any of that, perhaps you have. This outside world is just a manifestation of what is going on inside, that's all. The spirit will be here when we are not here. Therefore, it is tied to something more powerful than us. Call it what you want. Again, I am not here to tell you what to call it; but you are going to come to that concept and that conclusion inevitably. Now, we can do this right now and let's do it in the way you would like to do it as though you were home alone.

Second part As explained previously we are going to take it in steps. These steps are mind, body, and spirit. You just did spirit. This is your mind. In this book, there are spaces to write these answers, and you will write them because when you come back, there is accountability here. Does that make sense? This is coaching. This is not therapy. I do not care what your parents did to you and how you feel about them and why the dog kicked your bowl over. It is in the past. Who cares? What I care about is this: What are you going to do about now, moving forward? That I can help with.

Homework – Week 1 – Coaching:

Do you know what your three greatest strengths are? Chances are you do not. So, when you are in *stillness*, ask yourself, "What are my three greatest strengths?"

- _____

- _____

- _____

What is your favorite way of sabotaging yourself and your goals? Most of you have done it; every one of the people in your organization are doing it. The people who are not in your businesses yet, they're doing it too. They cannot get out of the box. They are still in it. You guys have at least said, "Well, I am thinking outside of the box. I am challenging the box." The people who are not there yet are still in the box. So, how do we sabotage ourselves? That one is also going to scare you because you are going to have to look into the abyss. When the abyss looks back, the character of the person is revealed. Let's get it out in the open people because we all agree that we're all messed up, right? So, let's deal with it, find the cause of it, change it in our unconscious mind, and free ourselves from our limitations. Wouldn't that be an interesting concept? If that does not get you excited, check your pulse!

- _____
  _____

What are you most excited about now? The possibility/the ability that you can heal yourself? Those are almost identical things. Isn't it interesting that we all want the same thing? We are all looking for peace. Now, each of us, over the next five weeks, is going to find it. You will experience it at least once. How many more times you experience it beyond that is up to you. I cannot guarantee that, but you will experience it once. When you experience it that is the moment of choice. This is what is called a: MOG. That is where the spirit goes.

- _____
  _____

That brings us to this: What three things will you do differently this week with this new knowledge you have learned to reach your goals? Now, you are probably thinking, "What goals is he talking about?"

- _____
  _____

- _____
  _____

- _____
  _____

That is the third part of the homework. What three goals do you have for this week, just this week? Keep it simple. What do you want to do? Maybe for some of you, it is able to get through stillness. I can live with that. I did not say it had to be business goals. You may have thought that, I did not; although, it would be interesting if you made it about your inner self. I still think life is about people. So, the quicker you learn about yourself, and you learn about people, the faster those external goals about life will pop up just like that.

Now, what is really interesting is this statement right here: The road before you is hard, black, and white. "It feels hard. It feels black and white." They either say, "Yes" or "No." "I am struggling. I cannot figure out how to get to the next whatever it is, the next level, whether it is executive, regional, president, or whatever. You get stuck, right? So, it looks black and white. I see the road, but I just cannot quite get it. It does not look as bright to me. It does not look like a possibility, but there is a way to change that road to living full color and your life out loud.

General psyche training

In the last part of this chapter let's discuss the change in perception to the smooth, limitless, and in full-color possibility by considering these different points that come to mind. Maybe you see the road in full color. Notice that everything behind your past pictures has disappeared. It was enveloped in your possibility, not in your limitation, with ultimate truth. The choice is up to you. I have offered you the invitation. I can do no more. I can show you the process. I can show you what I have done with thousands of people. This is all I do. From here forward, it is up to you. The question is: What do you want to do with it? Are you still thinking about the three goals for this week? What are your three goals for this week that we can all come back and then we can step back and say, "We have to trace the process actually, how they were actually accomplished?"

So, we created what is called a *"neural map" or "model" or "breakdown."* Where did the conscious mind intervene and from where did the limitation, fear, worry, and procrastination come in? Where did those other programs come in that we call "voices?" Where did they come in? We can alter them; and, by altering you, we alter everybody at the same time. So, *"What do I mean by goals?"* It does not matter, what I mean and what about this? If I tell you, I am putting you in my box. If I just say, "What do you think?" You have got to figure out where the box is if there is one at all. You have to explore your imagination, which is what I would prefer you do, but it does not matter what I want. You can go as fast or as slow as you want to go. This applies to everyone who reads this.

Let's think about it for a while. I hope that you do not think about the three goals and their achievement to do this, this, and this. Chances are that is not the deepest truth because they tend to be reactions, which are emotional-based, generally meaning you are just jumping. You have not stopped and thought, "What is it that I really want?" We talked about this a little while ago. We do not know what we want until we stop and get still about it. Now, what our ego wants: Everybody wants to be rich, everybody wants to be successful. What we want is peace. Now, you can have financial peace, you can have emotional peace, but what is it that you want? So, I hope it invites you to sit back and just imagine. Maybe you have been doing business so long you have a habit of just doing business, just a guess. Food for thought. Maybe it is the revival, for lack of definition, to reignite that fire that once got you into this or that. Maybe we can reignite it one more time because sometimes it can wear you down when you get into the habit of things. Change your perception. It is an invitation. It is an invitation to get freedom and help other people do it with you. I am not talking about this utopian society; we are talking about real work. You are going to work, reader, for the next few weeks & chapters. If you do not like it, I'm sorry, but get over it, because what you did before did not work. Otherwise, you would not be reading this.

I am not saying my coaching is totally going to work, but it is going to do something different than what you did to get here. You cannot unlearn what you just learned, and there are weeks and chapters of invitations and information. Each week we go deeper and deeper and deeper. The truth here is "*change is constant.*" The illusion is that "everything is going to stay the same." That is not true. It is just like any muscle you have in your body if you do not exercise your brain and explore it and discover who you are, it reverts to smaller, already learned habits. Would you all agree with me who you were when you were twenty and who you are now are two totally different people? It is the same body and yet you are a different person. How is that possible?

Non-exercising: of the imagination and the exploration of self that has allowed us to fall into the "humdrum of habit." We are bored stiff, and it is amazing we even get to that space. That is not life experienced. That is life passed through. Your heartbeat goes up and it goes down doesn't it? It has a little bit of rest, and it goes up and it goes down. That is actually a metaphor for life. Sometimes you rest, and you just kind of cruise. Sometimes you are climbing up a hill, and other times you are flowing downhill.

End: That is the end of our first week and its homework. By the way, the moment of grace = MOG. MOG is short for *moment of grace, for your recollection*. Moment of grace, in our world, means this is where spirit and the outside world sync up. There is no signal. I am aware of that. Your spirit, your gut, whatever your religious structure is, your deity structure is, again, it does not matter, provides a feeling, hairs raise on the back of your neck, or you get chills, or however it represents itself to you, is correct. Your spirit wakes up when you have that strange tingling and you get the chills. This is a MOG. That is where your spirit is saying, "Wake up. There is a choice here, but *you* choose."

The truth is spirit has always giving us the opportunity to choose. Spirit is not here to condemn you or to tell you that you are a bad person. You do that enough on your own. Spirit does not need to help you. Spirit is here to give you an opportunity to become whatever it is that you want to become, and it gives you opportunities to choose what it might view. You might not choose it, but it is always going to offer the invitation. It is going to keep coming back around. "Do you want to be free?" Otherwise it will wait for another opportunity to choose, which is what we control or our freewill. Every deity structure has it. We have freewill. "God gave us freewill." "Yep, he did freewill in eating, sleeping and all other things that we want to do. Some people consider it as unimaginable, but He did. We have a brain that is ill equipped for the task and the responsibility, but he did. Thank God he did. We can choose not to participate with the MOG or follow it, which is our choice.

Maybe we are the reverse. My *entire objective*, in the five weeks here, is to teach you how to *identify MOGs* for what works for your spirit and what jives with you. So, as you walk around, you do not have to do anything. You just stay awake and watch and enjoy your life. When you meet the person you go "click", by introducing, "I got something I want you to take a look at." That person says, "I feel you. We're in." It has nothing to do with the business itself, is Spirit syncing. Get over the business. It overwhelms people. This is what I see people doing and it overwhelms them, stay simple in connection and it will open many doors.

So, bring it back down to what got you into your business. Bring it back down to the basics. Use the psychology here, so that people see it and more importantly their Spirit "sees" it too. It makes it a whole different ball game, and one that is fun for everyone to play.

CHAPTER 4

Architecting360 Training II
(Thoughts, power and Effects)

This is psyche training part two. In this chapter we will understand how the mind works, more deeply than prior chapters. So, basically we are going on to *Step two of the Architecting360 method*. We are going to start changing how your brain perceives and the way it thinks!

Questions to Ponder:

- Did you do "stillness" last week?
- Did you do it more than two times?
- Did it happen every day?

Let's start with the basics: The conscious mind never shuts off. We are going to learn how to use that in this session. What else did we discover? It is funny how the biological clock works, right. Have you started to notice that you can keep still? You actually can do it and maybe that sounds odd, as it is something that you have to discipline yourself to do; because, if it is left unchecked, it will not become a full lifestyle habit. We are almost kind of like those affected with Tourette's in our "knee-jerk" mental responses, thoughts, and emotions. So, we can imagine that environment affects us, too. As we discuss in the homework, about stillness, we talked about, "**Pick a place.**" Part of that is to set you up so that when you walk into that "place," as soon as you sit down, your mind/body feels & knows that is the place, and it is time to get still, immediately. We have not gotten into this yet, but it is called an "***emotional-physical anchor.***" Let's have few examples

- When someone walks into his office, what does he do? Work.
- When someone walks into his living room, what he does? Watch television.

This is designed for us to pick a place/environment that is our "space" for these particular activities.

Next step: What was the longest time you found that you could stay in stillness and how surprised were you? Twenty minutes is about the average. You will notice that it is going to get longer. It will do it all by itself. The reason being is what we are going to expand on, how that works for us in this week's session and the following, subsequent weeks/chapters. It just gets us to identify that change is necessary. Let's start finding where the *limitations* are. Most of us are afraid to look at the limitations, because if we look at them, we have to admit that we are living them. That is exactly where we need to go first, to remove the limitations, because naturally we are already limitless. That's the logic here.

What prevented us from going inside during stillness? Examples might be, the environment, children, finances, and eighteen-hour workdays (more/less); there is not enough time in the day, etc. Sure, it is hard to stay focused. So, when you are talking to people and their head is going one direction, and their mouth is saying something else, something inside is not agreeing with what is going on. It is like two minds arguing with each other. It is called *"subconscious incongruence."* Here the point to remember is that the subconscious cannot lie. It is not a liar; That would be a conscious thought and the choice to embellish. What else have you noticed that has prevented us from going inside? Everything is a distraction. A nose itch, face twitch, and itches in places you have never had before. We are all the same in our conscious minds. If you want to analyze yourself, you are attaching a thought, because that is what this week is about because we are so busy being in control or, worse yet, having the illusion of control!

Discussion about homework (week 1)

Beliefs: Readers you do not have to tell anyone all three, but let's agree for the next couple of training rounds you are going to honest. It doesn't matter that you made mistakes in the past; to be successful you have to be honest with yourself first. If you want to share something about your beliefs or thoughts, forget the idea that you are embarrassed, because if you are thinking it, chances are that somebody else is too. If you are going to lead people, you have to be willing to speak your guts. You had to create *three* new beliefs for us to move forward with our lives and this *Architecting360 Training Program.*

We need to trust ourselves and have confidence in ourselves, right? You can't project it to others and expect them to believe it when you do not believe it on the inside. You are either a good BS'er, or you have not accepted where you are on the inside. Thus, there is also an integration sequence happening. There is still that inner part of you; once we get into week four we will address it specifically (which is called *"Emotionality"*). So basically our goal for now is to be self honest-absolutely.

Let's have an example, if someone says "Hey, have you made any money at this?" Your first response is, "What do I say on the inside before responding? If I tell them, I have not made a freaking dollar…" or "Why the heck is he asking about that already?" Readers, it is because you have got the zealousness and you are excited and all of a sudden someone says, "Hey, by the way, let me rain on your parade," and you do not want to be rained on. It goes back to self-belief and deserving you are worth it.

Ownerships: This session we will talk about ownership being a big thing, and that is what we are looking for in our lives and businesses. We are looking for people who are willing to own it (meaning their lives). I do not mean like own the business, but own the responsibility that business comes second to living life fully expressed. We have got to get beyond our logical, conscious thought process, and get to the root of the matter; which is in the subconscious.

The first step: is actually about the installation of these new belief processes in your daily lifestyle. It is kind of interesting that you are placing limitations and really not aware of it. I did not say you had to stop practicing stillness or stop at ten minutes, but it is like the reserved seat last week. We have already created these *stereotypical limitations* of what we can and cannot do. Therefore, we have permission to break the rules, specifically those that are imposed by ourselves. The aim of this example is, "In business, specifically your own business, you have to be willing to take responsibility and not play by the rules, because the rules are made by the person who owns the business." He who has the gold makes the rules. In this case, you have both. It is conditioned from a previous mindset, maybe it is a previous job, parents, you don't know how to run your own business, or whatever that (mind) says, "Well, I am just going to only do what is necessary on the homework." I just wanted to see how far we could push. Readers you starting to see how we are going break some of those limitations already, right?

Second step: How did "try" and "don't" change your experience with life? Did you bust anybody on this, besides yourself? Did you call people out when they used one or both of those words? Did you notice how they responded when you said, "How is that *try* working for you?" It kind of knocks them off their pattern doesn't it? It is very entertaining. It makes it a whole lot more interesting, for sure. How did that change your experience to see beliefs in motion external from your mind? Is possible that it makes you just more aware of what is going on, and you start to notice the limitations? ***How our thoughts come in our head***. A lot of times, we will just spit out what is in our heads. We don't even know what the heck we just said and we just repeated what the person who taught you told you to say, and maybe they have limitations that we are not aware of etc, etc. It is our responsibility to discover them; and, for the world that you are creating, if you do not, you will continuously repeat the mistakes.

Basic Introduction

Implementation of beliefs: How do those three beliefs (homework from last week) need to be modified and implemented in our daily lives? It happens automatically. Ask the question to yourself and close your eyes. Go into stillness (read this part first and then go back and implement). You know how to do it by now. Listen to yourself and see what comes up. You do not have to think anymore. Thinking, we have already proved, is a dangerous process, because it has rules. While you are in stillness, wouldn't it be interesting if you just relaxed a little bit and got ready to receive what is coming? Would you believe one minute has already gone? That was one whole minute of your entire life. How many of you feel that you are not ready or not finished here on the planet? There is still more to come, right? That was easy. Now, what if you started implementing this? Now, I said roughly ten minutes a day. Did I say when and how? Of course not. I did not say that you had to do all ten minutes at once, right? It is a nice little setup. I told you last week that I would constantly be testing your heads to break the limitations. You do not have to do the ten minutes all at once. You can choose to, if you like. When you get the chance, just stop, at a lunch break maybe, and just do five minutes out of your day, or while you are at a street light waiting for the light to turn green, just stop, even for 10 seconds or 15 seconds. The faster you do it, the neural network in your mind, the actual neurons, create a faster and faster-growing subconscious habit. They literally jump faster between each other and the habit gets stronger. The more often you do this, the quicker you will be able to relax your mind and listen more to your Spirit.

Someone will let you know that there is another world out there, usually via his or her car horn! Sometimes it is very easy to get caught up in what our head is doing. We already discovered that in previous chapters. We will discover more in this chapter. It is nice to know that I can pull up the mechanism just for one second during anything that is going on. If nothing else, notice how your body behaves. You do not need medication to go to sleep. Now knowing what you know, what did you come up with and how do we need to modify it? Business, as we talked about in last chapter, and as we will see in this chapter, is an outward extension of what is going on inside the mind's business.

Now let's ask the obvious thing. We are going back to *limitations*. What stopped us from achieving these goals? I am sure you have more than three in your life. Obviously, we chose them. What stopped you from actually accomplishing just three goals, which goes back to self-worth?

- Procrastination
- Distraction

So, we know yours is a double-angle (Self-worth). Readers, we are going to dive inside.

Procrastination: This is very common. It is usually tied to a deeper belief. "I am not good enough" or "let me do the stuff that does not matter like sweeping the floor as opposed to calling this person." We all have to learn to say, "Am I worthy enough." Now where does that start? It starts with *belief*. Beliefs should be properly modified. If we cannot think /feel it, it is not going to show up outside. The person that is going to just walk up and "discover" you won't happen. It does not work that way. It is a 20-year, overnight success kind of thing. Look at my experience, I've been in business for 20 years but still I'm not there yet. Where do we perceive from? Your conscious mind right? We already know that it has rules, which was what last week was all about, *Foundations of Change*. We know the conscious mind has rules. Thus, if we continue to rely on it, we are going to be in trouble, the same trouble, again.

Greatest strengths: We already know about the weaknesses now. What is the strength that counteracts that?

- Independence.
- Loyalty.
- Flexibility.
- Teachable.
- Compassion.
- Passion.
- Commitment.

What is your favorite way of sabotaging yourself and your goals? (This is one of my favorite coaching questions) We have to look into the abyss, and it looks back, often. What do you have in you, doubt or disbelief? By creating instant and spontaneous chaos (Procrastination), we all should start working on our value a little bit. "Let me rationalize myself through this. I will talk myself right out of anything. I am my best counter-salesman." Procrastination is just an *externalization* of that internal value.

Well, you have to find out who you are. The cool thing about it is that you are constantly growing, or if you choose the latter, you are constantly dissolving. It just depends on what you choose. There is no such thing as static. We talked about that last week.

[**The last thing:** List three things you will do/want to do this week, differently with this new knowledge to, reach your goals?

_____

_____

_____

Placing Thought in Motion:

As we know from last chapter, the conscious mind perceives information on the outside world through our five senses. These are:

- Eyes (sense of sight)
- Ears (sense of hearing)
- Nose (sense of smell)
- Mouth (sense of taste)
- Hands / Skin (sense of touching/feeling)

We also know that as we perceive it through the five senses, we are filtering it based on our values and our beliefs. Examples: We will change what we *"think"* we saw. *Try* is another one. *Don't* is another one. *Should've, could've, would've,* which is a set of implied rules. More Examples: when someone says, "Hey, you should do it this way," what they are telling you is, "You should do it according to my rules." So, when someone says to me "you should," I say, "according to whose rules? Whose rules am I playing by, because *'should'* may mean something different to them, than it does to me." It is an unconscious trigger when you say, "Okay," because we are taught to follow the rules. Who made them? "Well, other smart people before us?" No, what we know is:

- ➢ We perceive information through the five senses.
- ➢ We know the conscious mind filters for the subconscious.

Here's where it gets cool: A conscious mind carries out the responsibility of choice and choosing what choices are made (so it thinks). Also we are going to get into this deeper. In the last chapter when we talked about the conscious versus the subconscious, the conscious mind is the deductive factor. It is what is reducing and filtering, to what works for you. It makes decisions all the time. It takes very little brainpower, but it is the only thing we have. You do have to be aware of the decisions that you are making. It is like what we discussed about a moment ago; different questions arose in your mind like:

- Why am I thinking these thoughts?
- How do they serve me?
- To what end am I chasing this outcome?

If we know the conscious mind carries the responsibility, who is watching the conscious mind make its choices? The unconscious mind is based on the auto-code that you start putting in it. As we go through this process, if we change the unconscious mind, it will naturally drive you to what you want. All you have to do is be awake enough to see when a *MOG* comes and follow it.

Readers, if you truly believe that we are all spiritual beings in some form or another doesn't it stand to reason just to follow the Spirit? We are all scared to death, and we do not talk about that. It doesn't matter whether you are Jewish, Christian, or Muslim (or whatever). You will be a better Christian. You will be a better a Jew. You will be a better Muslim. You will be a better **HUMAN**. You will be better because you are more in touch with the real you. I am not here to tell you what religion to believe. I am here to tell you that we are all connected, whether we like it or not. We all should agree with that by now.

We are responsible for our decisions, which means that we have to be constantly aware of the thoughts that we are thinking. Now, for some of you, that is going to blow your mind, because we are generally just cruising around on "autopilot." We get up, brush our teeth, get a cup of coffee, get in the car, turn on the radio station, pick up the cell phone, do our nails, etc. So on and so forth. We cruise throughout our day, get to bed, and then we are fried. Then, the fun starts, because then you start psychoanalyzing yourself saying, "What the heck happened today?" Better yet, because it is a linear mind, past/future, you jump into, "What do I have to do tomorrow?" You were asleep already all day. So, why are you worried about what you have to do tomorrow? Just go back to sleep. You are already on autopilot. Quit stressing out. I am obviously making jest, but you follow the point? This is the pattern that we do to ourselves, and we expect things to change. So, the conscious mind is responsible.

We subject ourselves to worry, doubt, fear, anxiety, and lack of choice by allowing the "Guard," (remember the conscious mind is called the "Guard"), to lull us to sleep. We allow it to put us to sleep, and then we get pissed and blame something external. Now, we blame ourselves when we become aware, but you do not have to blame yourself. **Blame** is a wonderful way to get into trouble. That is a self-worth issue, which is an auto-coded program that says, "I am not good enough. I am not worthy enough. So, I am going to keep finding ways to kick my own butt, and then I am going to externalize it, so that I can validate my internal belief. Before you know it, I am a joke." So, we create the auto-code. The auto-code shows up, and our conscious mind is just making decisions. Most of the time, we are not aware of what we are making decisions about because the auto-code is driving it. The subconscious is just a big computer. So, until we change what the auto-code is, we cannot make different decisions very well. About ten percent of the time, we could interrupt ourselves, but that of course leaves ninety percent that we do not.

Thoughts have the power

The trick right here: We must now become aware of our every thought, for they are the ones that have the power. The thoughts from the auto-code, we will ultimately change, but right now we need to start identifying what we are thinking, which is why I had you do the coaching questions. I did not put any rules on them. You did, and you may wonder why things are not going as fast as you want them to. It is not the pitch. It is not the product. It is not the money. It is what they are getting from you. All of the sudden you are finding a kindred spirit who feels like they do not have any internal value and they say, "You know what? I cannot sign up for your idea/business/plan. I do not have the money." Where did that come from? Come on, reader, we live in a communication age. I mean, we have cell phones and the Internet. How can we not talk to somebody these days? The result is that the thoughts have the power, being aware of them is the key.

As we are on this same point again, everything was thought before it became an internal or external reality. We are still human beings. We are just saying something different, in the above example. Some these of the things we will need to go forward, as the subconscious mind perceives things differently.

Structure of mind works: Let's have a review of structure of mind at an unconscious level. Do you have any idea that how many of people get chills, Déjà vu moments, or coincidence moments, and how do they know those moments are different? These are actually *Feelings*, that come from inside. It is attached to a different place beyond our awareness, beyond our conscious perception. The subconscious mind perceived it.

Where is that intuition coming from? The auto code is talking to you. It is saying, "Hey, listen up." If we already know that the consciousness mind perceives in filters. It stands to reason that you have to be mindful of what it is filtering and how it perceives. We have got to go a little higher. If 95% of our power is unconscious, why do we expect a big change of the conscious mind? It is almost insanity. Some of you have probably felt that way and maybe you do now.

Subconscious Mind

All of our "*trust*" ideas come from within the subconscious mind. Now, we are going to take that one step further. The subconscious mind in this particular analogy is synonymous with Spirit at the same time because the mind is the operating system. Recall, the mind is the operating system; the brain is the hardware. We do not know where the mind is. It is like the wind. You know it is there. It starts and stops. We cannot grab it or control it, but we know we all have a mind. Even if there is no brain in the head, we still have a Spirit in it. That is why it is called brain-dead, not mind-dead. Mind-dead doesn't exist. So, if we perceive well, our truest ideas come from inside. A good idea on this is how to talk to somebody, how to do the business meeting, or how to get people to come to your party/event/presentation etc. We normally don't think of that because it goes back to self-trust and we need to learn to trust our instincts again. Before we became logical creatures and stopped being Cro-Magnon, we had nothing but instincts. "Dinosaur comes running, got to go." "Let me think about how fast he is running times the square root of B, inertia, and momentum." Thinking like that second man would make him food.

Fight or flight: is a remnant of the reptilian brain, and we all have a reptilian brain. It is at the top of the stem. It is the oldest part of our brain as we developed through the evolution of man. It is still transferred down because we are all connected, because the structure of the brain is the same. Some a little uglier and some nicer and perhaps one has a little hole in it, but they are still the same shape. This week, as you start to do more of this, start looking for the ideas from within, because every answer you have ever needed is already there. We are the ones stopping ourselves. I know you do not want to hear it. I know your egos say, "Well, no. It is the economy. It cannot be me. It has to be the President. It has to be the government. It has to be this or that." It has to be something external. Some of the greatest fortunes in history were made during times identical to now. It is the perceptional shift of what is out "there" versus what is not.

Limiting mindset: Every work is difficult. Money did not just pop into existence. We invented it. It is just ones and zeros on the computer. Now, if you will notice, everything is starting to pressure up. Watch the attitude shift. Mark my words, over the next few months, everyone will be saying, "We feel good. The stock market is seeing new all-time highs. We feel safe." Now, people are going to start moving forward and investing deeper, seeking more. Watch, and the cycle will start all over again. This is nothing new. If you are older than 20, you may feel the fear of revolution. There are people who have, and there are people who do not have. It has nothing to do with the money. There is plenty of money on the planet. It has to do with the mindset that draws it to you. If you could start thinking about money as energy, as a concept, as a thought, or as a construct in your mind, different than something you hold in your hand. It just goes to her, to him, and it keeps going. It may come back around. That is why people mark the bills, to see if it comes back because the money is energy. Have you ever dealt with somebody who you know was trying to sell you something? Not just sell you something, but also they were desperate. You could tell that they just need the money. They did not care about you. They needed the money. "Hey, man, you have to do this. This is awesome. You have to get it right now."

It is *knowingness*. It is intuition. It is stopping and being in tune with you. What is going on here inside, not what your conscious mind filters? I can only help you tweak your filters. Watch. Don't think of the color red, now. You just did it. You know it is coming, and you still cannot stop it. How is that for scary? It happens. So, we cannot control our conscious thoughts that way. We can observe them and choose not to participate with where the thought takes us. That is the trick. Do you feel the smoke, coming out of your ears yet? The subconscious never sleeps! Thank God for that. Isn't it nice to know that you have a mind that runs your body for you? If we had to make our heartbeat, control digestion, or bloodstream, we would never get out of freaking bed. Serta mattresses would be happy, right. We would never even move. Just moving my fingers this takes more conscious brainpower than I possess, but all I can do is make the decision, and the unconscious mind activates it for me. Now, I trust it. It is still me. Why won't I trust my decision-making ability? That is your ego talking. You are going to make mistakes because you have to learn to trust you. We are still doing that. It is amazing. We are in the middle age, and are still saying, "Do I finally trust me? No, I trust you, because we have been friends a long time, but I do not trust me. You make the decisions." When it goes south, what am I going to do? Blame him. Have you ever heard that friends and money do not go together? I think that is completely moronic. It makes no freaking sense. "People do stupid stuff for money." Well, perhaps then do not do it for money and let's get different results.

Imagination and Spirit: Imagination combined with spirit can create whatever we want; it may be good or bad. Now, we are going to get into good or bad, because good or bad are constructs in our minds, because everyone of us has a different version of what good means and a different version of what bad means. Therefore, good and bad are simply subjective constructs, which is a nice way of saying, "It is up to you whether it is good or bad." I cannot tell you what is good or bad, but you have got to start identifying the thoughts in your mind that limit you from where you want to go and keep you down. I am not in your head 24 hours per day, which is a good thing for both of us.

Moments of Grace (MOG):

Through the subconscious, you will "see" and experience MOG's – Moments of Grace! In the last chapter we discussed a little introduction about MOG's, now we are going to go more into detail. It is quite possible that some of you readers have no idea about MOGs. *MOG's* are Moments of Grace. Now, I am not here to tell you what religion to believe, but every religion has the deity structure in that God will show up. If you want to get technical, God never left. *You* just checked out for a while. If you grab the concept of God's omnipresence, God is in everything and outside of everything. Therefore, everything is God. Do we agree on that concept? Whether you are Christian, Jewish, or Muslim, it does not matter. Buddhist, Taoist, Metaphysical Mind, Spirit, it is all the same. Call it what you want so that you can compartmentalize it, which is interesting. As a side note, we try to compartmentalize God. That is the most arrogant statement that I have ever heard made by an ego, but we do it every day. We are all guilty of it.

What is a Moment of Grace? Déjà vu, chills, or when all of a sudden a "coincidence" happens. You are sitting there driving your car and all of a sudden the perfect song comes on. You say to yourself, "that song was exactly the one I was thinking." It made you feel different instantly, didn't it? The funny thing is: We do not even have to know how it works. We just know that it works. Acceptance sometimes is the difficulty; because, sometimes the very thing that is going to solve the problem is right here in the center of your chest. It keeps putting it in your face. Saying look, just stop and look at what is happening and then once you have looked at it, then make your choice.

Where do you have to look at it first? Here, go inside and listen to your gut. Fate calls, "Hey, I think that Sue is going to call me today," and presto! Guess who calls? "Hey, Sue, how are you? I knew it was you." What happens when you start to see moments of grace is you do not have to be so freaking participatory with your conscious mind. You do not have to be worried. If all of us believe that we are Spirit-based beings having a human experience, why do we sit here and fret so much? Do we think that God forgot about us in some form or another? Do you think he said, "Ah, you know what? I like those people, but I do not like you people." Oh, say it isn't so. That is a limitation of someone else's mind. We already agreed. We just did it five minutes ago. If God, or whatever your version is, your Spirit, is inside and out, omnipresent, he is always there. Guess where he is? Right there in your chest. That is the intuition.

I have been a coach/guide for twenty-one years, and still I cannot tell you how I know it. I just know it. I just know that a person is going to call and they call; I feel it. The different is: "I am willing to stop and say, "*MOG*." That is where the choice comes in on your part. Now you get to decide your path. If you can identify what is happening at the unconscious level and see how it manifests, (It is always working on whatever programs are inside.), it is going to manifest externally what is happening whether you are aware of it or not.

So, if it is always working and never sleeping and it keeps throwing *MOG's* at you, maybe we should step back and pay attention. Wouldn't that be interesting? It makes life a whole lot more entertaining, and it takes a lot less energy. "Now, are you saying I am going to walk around thoroughly euphoric?" No. Even *MOG's* can happen on the non-positive results side. You can have things that happen to you, and you say, "Oh that is a Moment of Grace.

Now I know. Now, I can make a choice to participate in that bad experience/that bad thought process again or not." I keep saying, "Now that you have this information, what will you do?" Now, I am going to ask you a trick question. We all agreed at the end of five weeks you could go back to what you were before. Well technically that is impossible. You can *try* to forget all this. *Try*, but it will not happen because your brain is starting to expand. You are looking at things differently, even if you never hear from me ever again from this moment on. Just the information that you have already learned will start to change you. Just the word *try* will stay with you for the rest of your life. Just, try to *try* and forget that word.

First difficulty: Let's get real. Most people are too scared to realize their own dreams. Your heart is not an accident, yet some people will simply not follow it. Sometimes when people start following it, it's too late in life, and often they go backwards and seek to recreate a time, commonly called a "mid-life crisis." However, who they were then and who they are now are now the same person even though they share the same body.

Question: If you were to live your life fully, what change/s would make now? How many of you agree that you are not fully living your life right now: Mind, body, and spirit, emotionally, psychologically, sexually, and connectedly?

If you were to fully live your life, what change(s) would you make now to get there? Think about this for a moment. It scares you when you can finally have what you want, because you have to be responsible for it. What is it you want? Start with that. Fully live your life. I mean, the big stuff, not just, "I would like to have my house, and car paid off. I would like to be making $10,000.00 a week off my _____," as an example — even bigger dreams. The only limitation is limitation itself. We have got to be responsible for our own success. What change(s) would you make right now? Maybe it was reading this book. We will see the proof in the pudding because knowledge and wisdom are two different things. Now, be mindful, though, that you will create a limitation that says, "I can only go forward when I have done the whole list." It is not going to happen overnight. It might take a few years. There is a limitation right there. See how that works? Just be mindful. I am not saying that is going to happen, but if you are *analytical*, we just need to recognize them.

What could we work on right now that would make the biggest difference in your life? Part of you is going to say, "We are already doing it because we are here doing this multi-week experiment." I already know the outcome of this, because I have done this type of training a lot. I know how it works. I am interested in seeing how it works for you. How do you get past overwhelm? Let's start simple: What is overwhelming us? Why do we create chaos? It distracts us from doing what we need to do. What are you distracting yourself from? Right now you are looking for the answer. Where are you looking for it? What have we been talking about this whole chapter/week?

Going further inside: We already know that we all are messed up. But, if we *don't* get rid of the limitations and we *don't* go inside and we *don't* look in the abyss, then we are doomed to repeat many patterns. Now, from here forward when the abyss looks back, you can simply look at it, you do not have to participate with it. You can say, "Oh, you know what? I do not have to feel that pain anymore. I do not have to carry around that emotional baggage anymore. I choose not to participate." Some people will say, "Well, you do not know what my childhood was like. I do not want to know, as it really doesn't matter." If you keep reliving the past with the knowledge that you know now, you are for sure challenging yourself. You will be emotionally stunted for the rest of your life. Not my rules; Spirit's rules.

When we had the number three online show on Stickam.com, on the Internet and what we talked about on a particular show most people were uncomfortable with, it was called ***Dark Days.*** What do you do when the emotional, psychological, or spiritual dark days come? Watch TV for distraction. "I do not want to feel bad," you say to yourself. Maybe you are supposed to? Is it time to cleanse yourself out of what is making you feel bad? There is an old saying that says, ***"Disease is dis-ease."*** We are dis-eased with ourselves. Since you are stuck with yourself for about a hundred years, maybe you ought to look at that. Sitting back and keep getting the same result and expecting something new to happen is insane. You already know that one. It is the oldest one in the book. More specifically, keep doing the same stuff and waiting for things to change. You can rationalize and excuse yourself of a lot of it. "I did Fox's stillness, and I still cannot change." Now, if you are willing to look at it, the funny thing is, peace starts to show up. You start to experience peace while you are in stillness, just that calm. "Where did that come from?" It was always there. You did not buy it, nor can you. I promise you that you did not buy it in a mall, and you did not buy it at Wal-Mart, even though they are surely making you think they have it. You may think, "Back up a little bit. You are getting a little heavy there." Do you understand my point? We are afraid to look into the abyss; because, when it looks back, we have to recognize that this is us. That is the biggest thing to make a difference in this world. We all agree that we are a family for the weeks (chapters) we are here together. After that, we can go back to being distant or our prior selves if you choose.

Externalizing

Let's start with the basics. It's all about, what we like and what we don't. How about procrastination? Isn't that an interesting concept? What are we nervous about? What makes us nervous? Where do we feel unvalued and what do we feel? What thoughts go through your mind when you feel those feelings? According to whose rules will you say it's right? If they are your rules, then they are always right.

You tell me if they are your rules, only you can truly know. It is called *externalizing*. We are so consumed with what the other person is thinking. Heck, we cannot even monitor our thoughts. How dare the arrogance for us to think that we can do that for another person. We all say, "I know what he/she is thinking. I know what you are thinking. Not really, but it sounded good, doesn't it." What stops us from being, from just stopping and saying to another, "You know what? I am nervous. I am not good at this yet, but I am going to be great at it. I would like to show you something if that is okay with you." When we get to that level of honesty and awareness, amazing things start occurring without effort, MOG's are everywhere.

Beyond the thought: In every one's life there is a part that we do not like about ourselves. Everybody has it! Every one of us is light and darkness. Any way you slice it, it does not matter what your religion is, everyone has it. Otherwise, you would be walking on water right now. I promise you that all of us will sink. I tried it this morning, and it did not work out too well. Going beyond is about simply Being versus Doing, which is against everything we have been taught until now.

The Biggest difference: The biggest difference is *choosing* to be different than we are "supposed" to be. All of you came here with, hopefully, no expectations. That is probably not true, but hopefully no expectation under the opportunity that you may learn something that you did not know. Hopefully, that has already happened. I believe that is the truth. Whether you do or not is irrelevant to me. Did you catch that? It does not matter whether you believe it or not. I believe it. If you choose not to participate in this experience, should I take it personally? No, this is the hardest question you are going to ask this week. I am telling you now only because it has been my experience of probability that when human beings can have anything they want, they do not have a freaking clue what they want. Humans normally think they know what they want because they have created a construct in their mind that services some other parts as auto-code like:

- If I am rich, they will like me.
- If I have fame, I can get free dinner.
- If I have security...

Does anybody know what "job" stands for? It stands for: "*Just over broke.*" You create your worth. It is consistent because you want it to be consistent. I am asking you to take ownership.

Let's have an example: When people ask what I want, I tell them I want freedom on all levels of existence. I want financial freedom. I want spiritual freedom. I want emotional freedom. I want freedom of love. Just when I think I know how to love unconditionally, I find that I have another condition that I put on myself. I want it all the way. I want to be willing to go so far out there that you can say whatever you want... within reason, of course. I am not saying go out there and say, "Gibberish." Say what you are feeling, not what you are thinking. I do not care what you are thinking. It is made up in your head anyways. I care about what you are feeling. Isn't that what we all want anyway? If we want a relationship, what do we want? We want to be connected. We are not at all being connected. We do not try. We do not get attached. "I will just do the barbecue, honey. You do the bills." Those are others' rules. They are not mine and hopefully not yours. Have you ever heard the statement, "I want it all?" I am the same way, because the truth is, you can have it if you want it. Now, the part that sucks is that you are going to have to face the part of you that has not gotten it. That is the part that we have to look at this week. We have to look at it. We have to interrupt that auto-code because that auto-code is like the New York Stock Ticker. It is going to keep constantly running. You have already learned that in stillness last week. Did you not? Do not take my word for it. You experienced it.

Spacing (discovery): *Spacing is creating gaps in the stream of conscious thoughts.* Now, we all agree that we have a boatload of thoughts happening at all times. When most of you go to bed at night, that is when you probably stop, because you have gotten all of the distractions out of your life and out of your way. Now, you can kind of look inside. Spacing is the creating of spaces in the random stream of constant thought we call consciousness. Even right now as we are talking about this, you are having a flood of thoughts coming through your mind. Some of them have relevance to what we are doing. Some of them are about all the stuff that we have talked about that is coming up already. Some you may consider it just crazy talk. If we all agree that words have power, then we must also agree that it is the "Space" between the words where the understanding occurs. More space, more peace, and that set us up for step three in the next session. The stream of consciousness is constantly going, it is on autopilot. How then do we create space between our thoughts?

Homework

We are going to get to learn how to do it now. This is in the homework too in case you forget.

- Step One: Do stillness first.

Why do we do stillness? Go inside, and check out what is going on. Get a little more peace from the outside world, via our inside world. This is the first thing we do. Do stillness for ten minutes minimum. Why ten minutes? You have probably noticed by now, after the first five minutes and your thoughts shooting around, and you finally calm down a bit, you can start to feel the peace. It is the peace you are looking for. When you feel the peace, you are there. That is all you have to do when you are sitting still, just feel the peace. How do you know you feel peace? How do you know when you have arrived there? You already know it, don't you? You cannot explain it. It is a *MOG*. We all have it. We call it: Spirit, God, or whatever you want to call it. It is up to you. I call it Spirit for simplicity. As soon as you feel it, that is your clue. Just look for it. Just sit back and wait. I mean, you are going to have a lot of thoughts go through your mind, people. Some of them will be just random stuff. They will go by. Watch how tight the stream of consciousness is. If you are like most, there are very little gaps between thoughts. They are just one right after the other one, rapid fire.

When you are doing a presentation, you are thinking about all the "what if's," and at the same time, you are *trying* to talk to somebody, *trying* being the operative word there. You cannot be a double-minded person. "The people that did not get in first are the ones that come around later, so I will just go for it later and later." Then you come around and say, "I have talked to everybody that I know." There are bunches of people that you do not know. If you know seven billion people, I would love to meet you, because I have met many thousands of people and I do not know everybody. So, therefore, it is a limitation and illusion that we create and say, "I have talked to everybody that I know." You do not even know yourself. So, how the heck can you say that? Come on. Let's be honest. Get real for a second. We do not even know ourselves. *You* have not even talked to *you* yet, much less everyone you know.

You just say, "Hi, have you seen _____." They say, "No, I have not. Let me check it out." You say, "Well, you know, if you are just paying your bills, it would be good for you to see it. If you want to make more money, you could tell other people. That is why I thought you would be perfect for this. It is a wonderful opportunity and we are all running out of time." They say, "I know." Why don't you practice on yourselves before you talk to somebody else and expect him or her to go? If you are lucky, you will get one of those that are like one-in-a-million that goes, "Hey, I get it." You say, "Yes! What do I do? What do I say, now that I am getting what I want?

I do not know. Nuts! What do you do? You get back on the search for another one-in-a-million. Rinse and repeat.

Illusion here: There is no end of the course, called life. You may not make it to the end of the course. That is an illusion. We could get on a plane tomorrow and die, and never get back. There is no tomorrow, people. That is an illusion of your mind. When will you do it?

See how it is easy not to make the decision? Let's just use an example: "I am going to do it at the end of the course." Oh, no, you know you will not. You can do it today. You have not done it, and it is already on your list from last week. I told you that the coaching started this chapter. So, if you are scared to get called out, quit right here, right now. I will not take it personally. If you want to change finally and get to who you are and make something of yourselves and be who you were truly designed to be, stick around, but we are going to go inside. You got me psyched!

- While you are still in stillness and your eyes are still closed now (You do not need to see this. This is all in your head.), imagine the number one (1). Now, you can pick anything that you like. I happen to like it simple. It is a no-brainer. Just imagine the number one coming from peripheral vision and stopping somewhere over your right eye.
  As you are sitting there, it comes over your right eye and hovers there. Now, it can represent o-n-e, or it could be the number 1. However you represent it, it does not matter. There is no wrong way to do it. Is everybody with me so far? Just the number one, just like you see on a screen. Imagine it stopping right over your right eye.
- Once you notice it, without a thought, say, "Oh, there is a number one there." Now, just take it a little walk across your field of vision over to your left eye. Are you with me so far?
- Now, taking your attention off of the number one, swing your field of vision back to your right. Now, bring the

number two (2) out of the field of vision so that it is over your right eye. So, if you are looking in the distance like a triangle, you will see the number one over here (left eye) and the number two over here (right eye). Now, the funny thing is, if you notice where they are, there is a big space right in the middle. There is a reason for that.

- Look left, look right, then center, and hold no thought for as long as you can. This is how we create space.

Challenge: For some of you, that is going to be a real challenge, because you have a stream of consciousness that is really tight. For some of you, it will be easy, but you have to practice it. If you can hold it there for three or four seconds, that is awesome! If you can hold it there for 15 seconds, you are godlike. If you can hold it there for 30 seconds, pish, then you are truly one in a million. It is challenging, but it is designed to be. Even those three or two-second spaces, start to break it up, they start to break it up just a little; because, if we do not break up the stream of consciousness a little bit, how can you put anything else in there that is ours? We cannot break through the walls of the castle unless we start chipping away at it. This is how spacing works. That is all that you have to do, just stare into space. See the one and the two, and just stare right in the gap. Just go into observance mode. Observe whether you are thinking or not.

You will notice because a thought will come up, but they are subtle. The better you get at this, the more subtle the thoughts will become. There is another one. "Ah!" So, how do you start over? Go back to Step One. One, two, and hold it. Keep training your thoughts. I told you from now on you could no longer afford the luxury of allowing your thoughts to run wild. You cannot, because we already know that the unconscious never sleeps. If a thought gets into the subconscious, it is going to manifest it. Whether it is what you want to manifest, that is the trick. This starts creating space. Next chapter, we will start putting stuff back in, which is called

"*Stacking.*" We will start stacking back in what you want. Now, all of a sudden, your auto-code is working for you. I will show you how to do that next week/chapter. So, you can stack it back in, and then your auto-code starts pulling you towards it. Guess what you do when you are out there and awake? You start looking for the *MOG's*!

Effects

Everyone has **effects** on one another. These may be good or bad, pending your point of view. If each one of you just affected one hundred people, what could we do together? For most people, it is exciting. For some people, it scares the daylights out of them, "Oh, no! I am responsible for other people." I did not say that. I just said you are responsible for you. I am the kind of person that promotes you now and then, but occasionally I will pop your/my chops. Imagine if we had popped our own chops five months ago, how much further along would we be. Recall, once you get there, and you have achieved that goal, your brain shuts off. That is why I told you that last week's goals are gone. If you did not get them, move on.

Do not fret about it and go backwards. No big deal just relax. Instead of saying, "Oh, I have last week's and this week's to-do," let go and focus on now. That is how you get too many things on the list of to-dos. If they were a goal, you would have achieved them by now, or you would have at least done the steps to say, "You know what? I am almost there. I honestly feel progress from myself, and I am comfortable with that." Otherwise, it just sounds good on paper. Are you waking up yet? Is everybody getting excited? Who is scared to death? If you said yes, you are one of the smart ones. Does everybody understand this process?

If you are starting to do this correctly, it will take about ten minutes, maybe one minute; because, after about one minute, it is just going to fry your melon. Maybe two. I am not putting a limit on you. I am just giving you generalization. Most people cannot make it more than about three seconds when they first start. The better you get; the more subtle thoughts become to notice. You want to become very aware of space, you are creating for yourself, as you do this process. You may think, "Okay, I am going to do my stillness now. What we are going to do now?" That is not what I mean. You have to make it a lifestyle choice. You do not have to stop at ten minutes. You can go for an hour if you want to it is up to you, just commit, do, and experience it.

It is time to start owning our lives. You know what we are so afraid of? Do you know what the number of fear in America is? It is the fear of happiness. "I am scared to death to be actually freaking happy; because, if I am happy, and he is not, I do not want him to feel bad." Let go of that, get happy. I mean it. If I am going to worry about his happiness, how am I going to reach him? Well, if I am going to reach him, I am going to have to go down into his world to get it as opposed to saying, "What would it take for you to come with me? I am waiting right here for you. I will show you how, together." It is an invitation versus a codependency. We are too co-dependent. "Man, I do not want you to feel bad because I am making a shipload of money and you are broke."

Who has been there? You know what? I used to feel guilty about having success and wealth. Guess what? I go over it. I earned it. I worked my butt off. It is not because I am a great guy. It is because I committed myself to it. I was willing to get money; but, then, when I got the money, I was bored out of my mind. So, I said, "What is it I am supposed to be doing out here, God? Now, what?" He said, "Talk to the people." "I do not want to talk to the people." I did not want to hear that. "I cannot do that," my ego/conscious mind said. My Spirit has other plans via my auto-coding that came in with me.

Follow your Spirit, no matter what the cost or what others think, it is worth it.

CHAPTER 5

Architecting360 Training III

(Showing the plan)

In this chapter I'll tell you the secret of sales. A sale is actually *Transferred enthusiasm*. That is all. That is what I invited every one of my clients, all the way from multi-billion dollar corporations to online affiliate marketers to experience and change their sales teams mindset. Readers, there is no such thing as sales. We don't have to convince anybody to do anything. In fact, if we try to, most of the time we will fail. The most important thing for sales business is the experience provided. It is just a transferred state of enthusiasm. For example, when we saw a movie, and we liked it, we share our feelings with others like, "Man this movie was great. You have to check it out." What is the difference in saying, "Man you have to see this thing? I am excited about this." Be excited about it. On the other hand, we get worried about what we don't like or get excited about, "*dominate thoughts condition your life.*" We are getting exactly what we are preparing our brain to give back to us. We create problems by ourselves, but we do not teach that in schools.

Here is the *challenge for the week*: You have to talk to ten people this week. No matter what you cannot lose or fail. If answer is, "No," they were going to say no anyway. If you think it is a failure, it is a failure. Would you be willing to say finally, "I get it?" Would you be willing to walk around and go out there and say, "I am blessed?" As a matter of fact, that should be the entire pitch. Walk up to them and say, "You know what? I am blessed. I have been blessed a long time. This business will make you feel blessed. Maybe that'd be a great pitch to affect someone, and your close rate goes up 20 percent, maybe 30 percent, or maybe more. It works every time as long as we figured out people by figuring out ourselves first. This is a people business, but somewhere along the line, someone told you that it is about this or that. It has shifted away from that very concept. It has become about money, retirement, and all these other things. You do not get them to change, make an invitation. We do not know their motivations, but the answer is very clear more often than not. It may be that they need self-validation. Maybe they are scared to find out that they are messed up too. That is why I am in the leadership training business, you know. We are all messed up, so let's work through it. Some people are not willing to do that, and that is fine too, but finding those who are is simple.

As we discussed previously, when I first created this program, it was 5-steps long, now there are many steps. This is just a good start. Here is a question for you reader: What do you think we study in every chapter? Were we having fun? If yes, why? I was not in teaching mode, although I was. I was just on a lighter topic. If you went back to previous chapter, the topic was totally different; that was called *Dark Days*. That is a very intense topic: *emotionally* and *psychologically-Spiritual* Dark Days. We hit that topic head on. It is a very **H-E-A-V-Y** topic.

Introduction

This chapter is about **the truth of light that shines** through us all. There is a coaching program, if you listen to the **Architect of BEing**^{TM} – **"Equipment to unwind your mind**^{TM}**" project**, which is the mother of all of our training programs. It is called: *The 1 Million Architects Project.* The project mission statement is going to reach one million people by Architecting more Architects, but it is going to do this by training the top 100 Architects in our methodology so they can make a difference because we cannot do a million people by ourselves.

Let's do it through the power of the cameras, but we cannot touch them as they aren't here, it's just an imagination at this point and all about what we feel about it, even when we do the big ones with 3,000 or 4,000 people; If there is a person way up there in the far seats, I do not get the same effect as I do with the person that is closer to us. I can get 100 Architects, each one of those Architects affecting 1,000 people, and we have got one million people just like that around the world. Wakes you up doesn't it? But "Waking you up", is another process here.

If our worst fears are "fixed," if we dive into it, I will coach myself obsolete. I am not your mentor; I am just an Architect and guide. You do not have to rely on me anymore. It's all about you. What you will do in the next few weeks, it will be up to you; I hope you are getting it. There are no rules except for the ones you create.

Goals of the week: The one thing, in this chapter we are going to do differently is to keep our word to ourselves and others; it is instilled in us from young age to keep your word, and If you do not keep your word, it's that "wrong" feeling you get that lets you know you are not being congruent with your spirit. It's just that plain and simple, so let's continue. If we do not have **T-R-U-S-T**, we are unable to do business with anybody. It is nothing personal and we are just not that interested. If you want trust, let's go. I am all about it. If no one trusts you, what is the point? That is food for thought.

Why bother if: We can't just keep our *integrity*? Why can't we, from the very beginning, as it seems too painful to tell the truth and seem less than "cool" or "perfect" or "in the know"? There will be people that will not accept this invitation and it is not personal. If you make it personal, you have to deal with the truth; it is not always about you. Give the invitation whether they accept it or not, and you can leave with courage. Just keep doing what you are doing and they might just notice. They might never notice; all you can do is give the invitation. That is it. Anything more is you trying to control what is never yours to control. You will be frustrated.

If it does not jive with my Spirit, then walk. Personally, my Spirit got dirty, and I said, "There needs to be something different here." We said, "This is what we do. We are going to stay congruent with our Spirit." It can wrap around whatever business / relationship because it is still about people. That is what the beauty of our business is, people, why do you think I am passionate about what I do? It goes anywhere, and it is always with me. We are all kindred spirits.

Stacking is your third session, stacking back in. Stacking is placing into our stream that which we want. Stacking is the placing of thoughts, fantasies, and desires into our stream of consciousness, but we cannot do that if it is one conscious stream continuously. This is why we created space. So, when you are in "space between your thoughts" as we did last chapter, then we start stacking back in what you want. By stacking back into our subconscious thoughts, we choose what we desire directly, versus indirectly. We increase our Light, our positive energy, and like attracts like, with *MOG's* coming more often. Moments of Grace; they start happening faster and faster for whatever your stream of consciousness is. This is the process of now stacking back in. It is a process, people. It is easy to replicate. I have been at this a long time. I want to guide you as a coach to do that, not as just a parrot that regurgitates, rather, truly "knows" what they are talking about. That is the danger of it because you are engaging with peoples' minds. There is a responsibility there because you are inviting them to be responsible for their choices. If you do not tell them the craft to do it, you are leaving them in nowhere land. If you take someone who has got deep, hardcore anxiety, is very frustrated, very worried and say, "You know what? I want you to jump right into the stillness. I am not even going to tell you how or why it works, just try to do ten minutes of stillness." Their first response is to *run,* because when they close their eyes, and they go inside, all the "demons" show up. All the "stuff" that they are distracting themselves with, running around, keeping busy, and doing whatever they do and inventing distractions, the truth at first can be shocking.

Mind vs. Brain: There are some inventing distractions, if we *make them* go inside without the anatomies of understanding what is happening in their conscious and subconscious, and mind vs. brain, they explode, and they run. So it is a process, and yes we can replicate it. Let's teach as a coach. That's what The Top 100 is all about. Imagine a psychological break, nervous breakdown, and panic attack. "I have got to run as fast as I can. I have to pack my bags. I have got to go." It's that kind of stuff that comes up and to their and our own minds, during these first steps. You can change you. It is a constant that change is always occurring regardless of whether we are aware; perhaps this time we can be aware and own our lives. The question is: What do you want, REALLY?

Stillness therapy

Start in stillness for ten minutes and spacing from one to three minutes, not fifteen seconds. Keep doing it. Add more space; punch holes in that brick wall of thoughts. You have got to keep punching holes it. Ask yourself: "What do I want?" When you're in that space, when you are sitting there in space, and you ask yourself what you want, it will show up just like that. If you allow it to pop right up, it will. As long as you have done stillness and you are sitting in space and you are staring at the nothing. You ask, "What is it I want now?" This is a thought, I know, but you have to activate the unconscious.

It will pop up, and then all you have got to do is look at it and decide if that is what you want to participate with. If it is, then move to the next step.

Fantasize therapy

We create a fantasy about it. What would that look like? Do you know what it would look like, if not create it as the creator of your life. It is created it in our Spirit, then head into that interesting, thing we call "*Imagination*," as we discussed in the first chapter. Everything is a thought before it becomes a reality. So, you already created the thought. Stick it back in your auto code now. Now, it becomes a whole different animal.

We actually create the imagery and already have the feeling. If you are willing, I want you to be successful, because that shows me that this process, yet again, works, and we have tested it everywhere. I am going to keep testing it. I am testing it through the media now because I want to see if we can transfer through a camera. That fascinates me immensely.

Once we "have it," in our mind what our fantasy is, what it feels like, repeat spacing again. Now, we can go back and instead of asking the question of: "What is it I want, you stick the fantasy back in the auto-code, and you just look at the fantasy. Just stare at it. You do not have to play it out. You do not have to expand it. You do not have to make it any more than it was. Just stick in there and stare at it, and let your subconscious absorb it. That is the difference. Let's go back. Once you repeat the spacing, have your space, put it back in the auto-code, you stack back in the blank spot your fantasy, and also it pops in your auto-code, and now that fantasy will pop up in your brain all day long. It lights up. You do not have to think about it. You do not have to make any effort. You do not have to do anything dynamic. You do not have to write little Post-It Notes on your mirror or all that "outside" programming you need to remember is clogging your brain. Just put it in your auto-code. Stick back in space that which you desire.

Find yourself

This is **the best part, in my opinion**. Watch for the *MOG's* and be willing to say "yes" when they come. So, when they come, and people come up to you say, "I really should tell you this business plan, but can also tell you a story. It is my script. I will tell you my story, and I don't care about business stuff. I want to ignite in you what I have found inside me so you have it too. When it happened, I was extremely successful. I was retired. I was worth X amount of million dollars, and I lost it all. I did not actually lose me. In fact, I found more of me, and I am looking for other people who are looking to find themselves and recreate the life that they REALLY want. This part should really excite you and interest you, and if it does, I am going to take about five minutes of your time. I will show you this business, this thing, and we can go or not." You can do this for ten people in an hour. That is a very quick pitch.

I think everyone should produce his own "story" video, personally. What else is there really to share but your story, your knowledge, and your wisdom and in that you will find your purpose is fulfilled almost automatically. This journey is worth taking, is it not?

You have to go through yours though, because these are in my story. I found most of them are very effective, however I want yours to be yours.

Bigger MOG: *MOG's* happen all the time if you are just paying attention. It is already there. You have already started to discover all these new things. It happens all by itself, faster and faster and faster. All you have to do is hold onto the ride and pay attention to what is going on in your head. That is it. It is a much more entertaining lifestyle, isn't it? You are not part of the system. Sean Penn directed a movie about it called "***Into the Wild***." If you have not watched the movie, I highly recommend you watch it. *Into The Wild* is a true story about a young man who did that very thing. None of these constructs made any sense, and he walked away from everything. There is a scene in the movie where he takes all of his money and burns it at the side of the road and just walks. He grabs his backpack and starts walking. I am sitting there saying, "Damn, I admire that guy. I do not have that kind of freedom, and I preach freedom. It saddens me, as I still have work to do inside myself." So, I got the movie and invited myself to look at what I was valuing in my head and what showed up was my heart.

This chapter/week is about ***creating pictures*** and **stacking** them back into auto code. Create the picture(s). Make sure it feels right. Let your Light shine. I promise you, it will happen fast.

MOG's will be everywhere. Readers you have had *MOG's* happen this chapter, some of you may find more than five, ten, or twenty. It happens all the time. Everyone has already seen at least three that I am aware of in this chapter. Look for them here again yourself if they are not coming directly to your mind.

When we realize we are not on message with ourselves, just go inside to get the same feeling and have peace about it. Sometimes there are things that should be changed constantly, because people keep changing. I keep watching. I keep changing. We keep growing and learning:

- We, (as a couple)
- We, (as a team)
- We members of Earth.

<u>Homework</u>

The people business is part of the *pitch*. That is what we discussed in the last session of training, and you called them out on it. If we do it, it is more exciting to know and tell another ten people or more.

If you are afraid to tell them that you are not making a lot of money, let's forget about it and move directly towards your earning. We are not guaranteed that we are going to make it next week. This isn't a sales technique. They are trying to test your metal as to whether you believe in your product. That is what the question is about. The essence of the question is to say, "Well are you making money at it?" It is a skeptical line. You can validate the question by just saying *all right*. Are you making as much money as you want at your job, if not, would you be willing to look at the possibility of making the amount you desire; because, last time I checked, the job says your boss says you are only going to make this amount, and "you don't get a raise unless I say so."

In this business, I determine my self-worth. If you don't want to take on that responsibility, That's OK; but I was willing to, and I thought you might do the same. It is just straightforward, and there are no sales in that. There is no team in this business, readers. You are all in it for yourselves. We are all in it for individual reasons. The only team is you, this Book, and I. Now I'll not suggest to you that you walk around and screw people, but let's not create illusions that are real. There is no team here. Surely we read in this book to provide a better guideline, but at the end of the session, everyone is going to go to his or her own way. A "team" is an illusion. Inviting them to their own journey, which you are paralleling, that is real, that is congruent, and that is honest. That is the purpose of this chapter, integrity at all costs.

CHAPTER # 6

Architecting360 - Training IV

(Stillness, Spacing and Stacking)

Introduction:

The third step is *Stacking*. It is two-fold, and we will get into that:

- One is discovering what we want.
- Two is being able to stick it into that wonderful stream of auto code that is constantly buzzing.

Stillness

The question here is what are we discovering about it now? Let's go deeper. There are few questions, I am going to write because I want you to keep looking at it and keep observing more acutely. What are you learning about stillness now versus in previous training chapters? It is easier because it becomes more consistent and now, you know how to drop in to stillness easier. The stream is slower, there are not as many distractions going on and it is peaceful, correct? So, we are becoming more efficient, not as distracted. How long are you staying in stillness now? Are you meditating for the absence of thought? Now if you are getting it, you can get to the place where you are actually in stillness, then you get the absence of thoughts, which is probably spacing for most.

For those readers who didn't do it every time in this session and those who are still in the ten-to-twelve-minute mark, it does not mean you have to go any higher or lower. What is preventing us from going longer in it? What are the distractions that are keeping you from it? Each week we have a person that we kind of watch, a person who is keying in and who is transitioning and who is changing because I am addicted to that "drug of change." Last chapter was a real interesting turning point for you because you got to get to the point of what this was about for you. It was about getting rid of those things that just tweaked you, and you are not alone.

So, we still realize that there is always going to be some limitation of your mind to this process, ok that doesn't mean we it will prevent us from the process. That is why I want you to look at the limitations, not because you are flawed. It is because we are still spiritual beings in a human experience, and it is not we "get it," and once you get it you got it. It is a constantly, evolving process of self-realization. We are going to learn through training session four, which is *emotionality*, the more you peel the onion back, and there is still an onion with smaller, thicker layer than the one prior. It is just smaller layers of it, but it is always going to be that way. When you become comfortable with the un-comfortableness of going, "God, I am never perfect; I never got it," then you can flow. Then, when the limitation comes, we may still get an efficient look and get the distractions out of my way but it will be much lighter; because, well, again, part of when we expel it, we may get more light in there. The light starts to shine, which is what we were talking about it in the last chapter, and at the end of the chpater you will recognize that it is most important.

Spacing

How many times this week did we do spacing?

Approximately what was the longest you held space between your thoughts?

Next question: How many times did you have to start over? Times. When I stop at the streetlight, I close my eyes, and go right into *stillness.* I can drop right into stillness. Hey, even if it is fifteen seconds, it's fifteen seconds more than I had where I could, at least, clear the mechanism of all the junk. Of course, it is a nice place to hang out, and yes you can start to interject into it whenever and wherever. It does not have to be where, "Okay, now I am going to do stillness," at a stoplight, close your eyes and quickly, drop in, check your breath, and go to spacing, even if you have only got fifteen seconds. It is just to create space, just to give yourself a break. For who is hardest on you? Of course, you, so give yourself a break, for a couple of moments for now and then beyond your daily routine.

We have talked about the stream of consciousness, the constant thoughts in your head that keep going; we know that some of that is auto-code. Spacing is designed because the unconscious mind has programs. The conscious mind is always thinking. It is always guarding and looking. Remember, we talked about that in the first training chapter. If you cannot create space in the auto-code, in the stream of consciousness, you cannot interject anything new or original. It keeps repeating itself; thus, this is why you always do, what you have always done, and you always get what you have always gotten.

Other multiple ways to do this: This is just one way I work people through the spacing exercise. This is just a simple way. The one-and-two is just designed to give your conscious mind something to preoccupy itself on. If the conscious mind is preoccupied, it cannot think. It has to look at the one and two. So, it has to hold its attention, one thought per second. If you stare at the middle of the 1 and 2, there is "nothing" there. Some people see white, some people see black, some people see gray, or whatever, but there is nothing there, hence, nothingness. As you get further into the *Architect in Training Program*, you will ultimately come to the conclusion and realize that everything starts from nothing, which ultimately comes, all the way from down here, Spirit. You start by going back to nothing, clear your mind and you stare at space. What ends up happening is because the conscious mind has to focus on the one and the two, it puts breaks in the stream of consciousness, like chipping away at a dam of your conscious mind.

Before moving forward to the next part of the chapter, which is **stacking**, those chips are little gaps where you can then stick back in what you want, not what is already there. If you are not aware, you are for sure on autopilot. When you see the things around you, you get aware of them, but your focus is here, Spirit. It is the same concept. One and two, but the focus is the dead center because you have to see the one and two from your peripheral point of view.

The object of starting at the "center" is that it keeps the conscious mind held and you can create from the space or center or Spirit. It cannot focus on more than one thing at the same time. If you do the break; you have a random thought and any which way you interrupt it, make it go back to the one and two, discipline the mind, stare into the nothingness. As we stare at nothing, it lets space in the auto-code and starts to chip away at the conscious mind, which is struggling to hold these two focal points, as it is not built for that anatomically. That is the effect spacing is designed to have. It is just to interrupt the stream of consciousness, nothing more. It is a step-by-step process and I found this out tragically. I used to come in and say, "Here are the five steps and we are going to do it all in the same session."

On average, it takes ninety minutes per session, and imagine if we did it all in one session, it might be difficult. Me with my team did a three-day workshop, doing this where we just did it in eight-hour blocks and people were simply overloaded. We had to keep modifying and chunking it down, so that you can get real results, understand the anatomy, the psychology of it, the unconsciousness of it, add *Spirit*, and give you a methodology that you can put your fingers on. Now, some of the things, esoterically, may not jam with you. **For example**, we may not know how a car works, but we know if we step on the gas it goes. We can either get caught up in the how the car works or just drive it, choice is up to you!

Stacking

A lot of people have questions about this, and all we have been doing is basically the same thing that we did the chapters before. Questions to ponder:

- What did you discover about "placing" back what you wanted into your auto code?
- How many times were you able to identify what you wanted and could put it in picture form or feeling form or hearing form?
- Did you get to that space?
- Did you have a hard time discovering what you really wanted?
- How did you get confirmation? (*Spirit*).
- How long did you stare at your "vision?"

I call it a *vision*, but that does not mean it necessarily is because it is going to represent itself, each one of you will experience it slightly different; but, you create the fantasy in your head like we talked about when we showed you how to create the ***fantasy***, and then you stack it back in. Now when you are doing spacing, when you are holding the one and two, now you put the image, the movie, the feeling, the thing, or whatever it is you want there in space. Now, your conscious mind is occupied by holding the one and two, but your subconscious is staring at whatever is in front of you. It then removes the darkness, because you remember you are filtering. If you get the conscious mind occupied, it cannot filter. Here, is a vision of mine, for example, that I have been working on for the better part of a year. If you are familiar with **Seattle and The Tacoma Dome** then imagine this, our goal is to fill the Tacoma Dome for free and host a *Architect360 Introduction Workshop*. When I am in stillness, after spacing this is what I am stacking back in to my auto-code, the dome filled with people all smiling and psyched to change their own lives. That is all you have to do to start any journey.

Author point of view: *You can change your life*, which is part of what the "Architect of BEing™" commercial, is about. When we do spacing and stacking in our minds, all we have to do is to see ourselves on stage, looking from my point of view, at twenty-five thousand people, saying, "I get it," and I just stare at that *vision*. Sometimes it is a movie. Sometimes I see myself walking across the stage. I see big video screens. I see all the people out there with these faces going click, click, click, click, click, and click... Sometimes it is just a still image where I am just staring from my point of view because then I am always looking through my own eyes. I do not "see" myself doing it because that is disassociation. I want me experiencing it, so I look through it like I am looking through my own eyes. I stare at it. We are one step closer, and we just *MOG'ed* it out. It just happens if you are willing to allow and believe. Questions to ponder:

- Do you ever wander off your *vision*?
- How many of you noticed the *vision* morphed as you were staring at it?
- This goes back to: "What do you want?"
- You start changing and then you have to interpret, "Are you thinking it, or are you feeling it?"

You have to become aware of where it is coming from and then as you get further into this, it is called **voice identification**. You start to identify the "parts of your personality" that interject things. That does not mean that you are schizophrenic, but we all are to a certain degree. It is just parts of your personality talking to you. That is why I write, you have to determine if it is your conscious mind saying, "Well, no, if I do this, it becomes that, and if it does that, I can do that." That is you taking control of it versus you just letting it come from *Spirit* itself or *MOG'ing* out. That is why we have to become very aware of your conscious mind at that point. You will notice if you break concentration, and all of a sudden your conscious mind starts wandering off and you are doing this or that, you must ask yourself, "How does it make me feel?" You have to go back down here because the *Spirit* is down here (gut area). Is it possible that what popped up was more powerful and more emotionally attached than what you were putting in there? Does that give you a sense of peace or no peace? But part of what is happening, too, is that you readers learn to identify that you do not have to know the *how* and the *why*. In fact, asking *why* more often than not pushes you back from what it was originally. We seek to control, but we never had control in the first place, consciously anyway. As we discussed previously about **CONTROL**, now the question is about "*why* and *when* is it going to happen". Sometimes it is tough, especially when it is something you want and you are desperately attracted to. The truth is all I have to do is look for a *MOG*, and that is where it becomes a little tricky because our ego jumps in and says, "Well, I can manipulate that and make it happen."

The only way to know for you individually is how you feel about it, because if the thought comes, you have to ask the question, "Is this coming from ego, or is this coming from *Spirit*?" The way that we start to identify that as part of this process here and what we talked about in previously, which is called **Emotionality;** where we start digging into the pockets of stored emotional stuff. The truth is that we do not have any control anyway. All the control we have is to choose, when it shows up, to say, "I have seen this before."

Let's have an example of a movie, *The Last Samurai*. At the beginning of the movie, one of the protagonists (Ben Watanabe) was sitting in meditation, and he saw a flag, then he saw a tiger on the flag, a white tiger, which is a precursor to a *MOG*. He does not know what that means. When is that going to happen and what is it that I look for? He stopped and said, "Okay, the white tiger." All of a sudden you see Tom Cruise and he's waving the flag with the white tiger and Watanabe says, "Stop," when they were going to kill him, because he saw the white tiger and said, *"MOG."* So, this is where you're unconscious and *Spirit* is now saying, "Hey, this thing that we were talking about that came through in meditation, here it is in "real time now, pay attention." This is what we are learning and now applying to our own lives.

It could be made to happen, just because the natural timing of things, which are perfectly done in *Spirit* and imperfectly done in humanity, we will muck it up, even though it feels really cool to get our hands dirty and say, "I can do this. I can make this happen." I will do this and that. I will move this piece over here. The reason it is hard is because our ego loves to mess with us; but, if you know how to mess with it, you can render it powerless. *Acceptance* is a good start. When I invite people in such a powerful way that they experience it, because I can do a commercial with you and you say, Wow, that is really great and you forget ten seconds later;" but, if I bring you into an experience, I give it away ninety minutes for free, and I put you in the experience and I grab you and you feel it, then you have an invitation. So, when we came up with the idea we could sit there and try to control everything as opposed to just saying, look, we just want to stand on the stage, look at twenty-five thousand people, and say, "Are you ready." That is all we stare at. So, in that case, it is an outcome. Now, when we did this training, it was very specific. I know exactly where I want the conversations to go. That is the variable and your homework is to collect different examples like that. Again, there are no rules, and be malleable.

Goals for Week Three

What were your three goals? How many did you achieve?

Some of your "goals" are really outcomes, which are never ending, versus a weekly goal, because part of what we agreed on for the chapter is that we were going to create goals for the session, and that was without outcomes. You can keep the outcomes all you want, knowing that goals once achieved will end and your mind stops focusing on them. The question is what stopped us from achieving all of them? There is process and structure that makes it happen and it does not happen by accident. Human beings are not random, but are creatures of habit. We are creatures of auto-coded programming. We already know that. We know how our *A-N-A-T-O-M-Y* works. We are learning how our sympathetic system works now, and we know how we are controlled, so to speak. Sometimes it stops us because we did not write down goals at all. In that case, one goal accomplished, because we had no goal. That is a perceptional shift by the way. Belief is a massive part of it. We talked about how "fear of success" is more intense than "fear of failure" because failure is what? It is definable. You know what is going to happen because we have done it a lot, have we not?

Questions:

- How often do we know what "not getting what we do not want" feels like?
- How often do we know what, "failure" feels like?
- How often do we know that we didn't get the goal that we set out for?

We become very accustomed at an auto-coded level, to "feel" like we have the intent of wanting a goal, really feeling comfortable with the intent, but never really delivering the goal itself, because we get used to the nine other times of failure, more than the one time of success. It does not feel good, but it does not have to feel bad either. Let's use that same number and extrapolate that. Let's take the random example of nine times we get a "no" and the one time we get a "yes." If you move that one time from one to four, does that extrapolate out success to you? It is not even half the time, and forty percent is still a good number. If you got forty percent of what you said you would do just a few steps ahead of were you are here, we still have evidence to prove that hearing "no," and not getting what you want all the time, the "failure factor," is still a 6:4 ratio. So, it is a very easy process to see that we are very comfortable with "no," because we can define it. As a parent, how often do you say, "No, do not do that," versus, "You can do that?" It comes from the stem of control when you boil it down all the way, which we will talk about a little deeper later; but it boils from control. At least, we can **control** how we are going to feel when we do not get what we want, right?

Subconscious: Let's move one step further. About the subconscious; if you aware that you are reading, you are "there" and your mind is somewhere else. There is another time and space, like here, but "there" is still in front of you in relation to time, it is always an illusion we deal with. I know that is conceptual, but if you step back and recognize that there is not a block to time and space except the ones we place on ourselves, there is no risk. Because what is the worst that could happen? Then there is no risk at all: but, beyond that, how about just letting go of the risk and just experience? If you agree, then we are on the same path. We all are ready to risk the failure. What about the reverse, success; you might risk that, "you might get what someone else wants." Then, what we do when we get exactly we want? All of a sudden we have to redefine what we want again. Now, we already discussed this earlier, you digress back into a habit that you can define, if you do not consistently redefine, whether it is an

- Emotion
- Action
- A relationship,
- Self-destruction etc. …

You will regress back to it because you can define that. It is maddening, but it is a habit and a program most of us share. Putting in the *Spirit* and *Light*, sometimes we get pushback, because the people around us may not want you to be happy. The more you shine; more people will want you to make you a little dirty. Have a look to few random examples:

- I am going to put you down.
- I am going to give you a hard time.
- I am going to call you a whacko/crazy/nuts/insane (been called them all myself).
- I am going to think you are foolish, and you are not going to be successful.

They are ruining your parade. "Oh, he is doing mind control on you," which is my favorite because, if it were mind control, all I desired would be done by you by now. Well, now I can define that I am apparently not that good at mind control. So, we know what is stopping us from achieving and part of it is the commitment, in and of itself. To commit to it means that we *have to make a commitment.* Now here is a *why* question. Why are we so afraid of commitment to ourselves and yet we expect other people to commit to us? That is just some more food for thought. Meditate on that one for a while!

Committing to ourselves: Ask yourself the *question*: "What is stopping us from committing to ourselves, because ultimately the truth is, who cares more about us than ourselves?" I do not mean disrespect to your significant others. They care about you, but at the end of the day, if something happens to you and they are still alive, I promise you they must go on. It is inevitable. If you care about them one iota, you would want them to, because otherwise, they are the walking dead.

There always has to be her and him, or there is no we, which I learned from relationship counseling. That was a long year, a very long year. He and she, or there is no we. So, the same thing; but, if we are not willing to commit to ourselves and say, "You know what, I am willing to do this. Even if our partner does not want to do it, I am going to do it for myself," even if you have to drag them along just by watching and leading with courage, and let them watch. Some of our friends are already doing this to us. That is why we cannot talk about this while we are going through it, as people will mess with it. They do not want your *Light* to shine unless you are going to dump it into them first!

You shine your *Light* at me first, and then I will support you. Until then, nothing is going to happen and in the end they may say, "Man, I don't know." However, it works that way out there. This is a nice little utopian world. Everyone wants to *complete* himself/herself first without caring about others. I am not saying that they are bad people. They just did not know what you know. Now, you can spot it. Then they commit one way or the other, and you know what you are dealing with. They may not know, but you do. That way you do not take on their stuff.

Why Questions:

There is a lot of *why* questions and what I call it the *"why"* loop. We have to get out of these *why* loops. Because *whys* become answers. That is why I suggest that they become loops or spiral-downs. If you have a *why* question, there is a *because* answer, which is probably going to be manufactured. It should be mentioned here because that is what this chapter is all about. This is personal coaching time.

Now, what do you want? Now you have been through five chapters of that. Now you know how to start placing into your auto-code. You have already noticed that it is starting to morph now. It is getting more and more defined. Things are starting to bubble up a little bit. I think maybe you are scratching off some of the old wounds from the list, scratching the old things off. We are getting some of these emotions out of the way. There may be even more to go. We know we have two systems that control our internal and external experiences.

1. Nervous system
2. Sympathetic system.

- The subconscious mind controls the nervous system. It is what makes our hands move, for example, and helps us relate to the external world. So, if I touch the stove and it is hot, my nervous system says, "Move your hand, because that is burning our hand." My Sympathetic System does not do that, but my nervous system does.

- My Sympathetic system is the one that goes inside and makes all of these wonderful little things we call "organs" run. It also helps us interpret what is happening in the mind, unconscious, and *Spirit*, or your *Light*, your solar plexus. So, the more *Light* we put in, the brighter the *Light* becomes. If you have noticed, maybe, this week as your *Light* started to shine a little bit more and you started to fill yourselves up, people around you started to change a little bit. You did not have to do anything. They just did it all by themselves. Now, we have to start to find out if others have their *Light* on or not. It does not mean they are bad people, it just is. You may notice you had other people that had their *Light on* that said; there is something different about this chapter training and you.

Most of us got that response or something along those lines. That gets people's attention. That would be a *MOG*. What did you do to get that response(s)?

Maybe you got comfortable in your skin, with yourself and didn't have to control as much. We end up putting our "stuff," on our partners far too often. There is an old saying. One of my early influencers used to say (Dr. Barbara DeAngelis), "What one partner suppresses the other one expresses." So, if you are suppressing control, all of a sudden they are expressing, trying to control. So, now all of a sudden you express acceptance. Maybe someone doesn't feel_____ (whatever), and says, "Hey, wait a minute, you know, I can relax." I can accept you, which is done at the subconscious level. You do not have to do anything. That was the ultimate thing I was driving towards. You do not have to "do" anything but choose; choose to be. It is effortless power versus powerful effort. It is almost scary because our conscious mind says, "That was too simple," when it is really that simple.

- What did I do?
- What are the steps?
- What is the stuff I am supposed to be doing?
- Was it stillness or stacking?

We start scanning. We go into fix mode. Remember, you are already fixed. The objective is to get ourselves out of the way for things that we created that appear fixed but are really broken. It is oxymoronic. I know that may feel odd and probably against everything you have been taught. We are already fixed and attached. If you just let it happen and let your *Light* shine, it becomes eerily interesting. The internal system (shine) gets dirty or clogged with emotions compressed or stuffed down. These are the two words you are going to lock onto this training session:

- *Compressed.*
- *Stuffed down.*

This session is going to scratch some itches. This session means the first half, because then we are going to twist you up with the second half right after that, again!

Compressed or stuffed down: This is the natural inclination of human anatomy. We do not deal with things or emotions; we stuff them down inside more often than not. You can have an emotional outburst, but you did not deal with the emotions that are behind that outburst. It has got to go somewhere. That is what's interesting; where does it go? When the system gets clogged, backup occurs. I do not mean backup like constipation, although, it is very parallel; the body starts to adjust and "hold on to" the backup. What do I mean by hold on to? (Weight, disease = dis-ease). In my opinion, most of these are from this occurrence, and even the medical world is starting to come around on this topic. It took them a while, but they are starting to get the hang of it that not everything is a pill-popping solution. That maybe a possible-neurosis situation has created a physical response. I wonder why that is?

So, the system, like any other, therefore must be cleansed to hear (which is hear, feel, see, depending on who you are), and for clarity and peace of mind. Now the peace of mind comes up (Spirit) and not down (mind). Most people think, "Oh, I have got to get peace of mind." No, it started here (Spirit) and worked its way up. It does not go to mind and work its way down. If it's on its way down, we are back to the mind holding on to distraction. You have peace here first (Spirit) and then it bubbles out, which is what you learned last chapter, which is why we go through systems so that people can learn it that way because that helps to understand and implement, piece by piece.

Let's talk about it a little further. Imagine the body acting as a glass container. Thus part of your visual imagery now is, as you start to go the S-S-S part, (Stillness, Spacing, and Stacking), let's start to imagine your body as a glass container. From here down (neck) is just a glass container. Start to conceptualize it. If you are full to the top, and I shake it, and I pull my finger off, what happens? Some people call that *emotional outbursting*. Some people call it *venting*. Some people call it *expressing themselves*. I call it *explosions*, meaning that the body has gotten so much compression in it and you have stuffed so much down, that it must be released somehow. If it does not do it, it starts to go back to the previous, which can develop into issues like dis-ease, which can be a plethora of things, and is not defined by any one person. It just shows up how it shows up based on the topic. So, what is stored in it is like any other container, except that our storage is not necessarily liquid, we might be talking about muscles and body weight. I am talking about emotional baggage. We are storing it. Thus, the body will, unless relieved of the "pressure" of its contents will "vent" reactively out of survival, and we lose it emotionally.

- Have you ever just gone off on somebody?
- Have you ever gone off on yourself?
- Have you ever looked in the mirror and cursed yourself out?

Now, here is the funny thing: It felt better for a while, and then the same pattern started all over again because there was just enough room in the *auto-code* to fill the glass container back up with the rest of the "Stuff" we had not dealt with. When you peel the top layer off, the next layer kept working its way up and you kept that stuff down. The body will adjust, expand, and it will hold it. Eight out of ten pounds of physical weight is emotional baggage, in my opinion. It is not what you eat and not how you exercise. I am not saying that you can eat a case of Oreos every day, of course, but if you look at when the weight gain occurred, it was probably around some emotional trauma. For example: a death in the family, divorce, the death of a dream, etc. Some trauma likely occurred. The emotions got stuffed and what ends up happening psychologically is (using weight as an example), the weight becomes an emotional trauma suit. It is padding. You cannot get inside now. You cannot hurt me, and I can push my weight around. We are not going to go too much further with that one, but you get it.

The *venting* is done out of emotional outbursts, words with wounding power and an "out of control" look and feel. Some people call it PMS. There is no bias of men or women here, it is just "**PMS**." Men have it every 45 days. We go a little bit longer, but then we lose it. We do. Most guys do not want to admit that, but, eh, its true just ask any woman they will confirm. *Words with wounding power* are the ones I want you to lock on because the "wounds of the words" are not necessarily external. It is the words that you hear in here (heart), your own mind that wound you. *Light* gets smaller each time compression occurs. It does not mean that the *Spirit* goes away. It just gets harder and harder for the light to shine through the mud. It is the lack of clarity if you will. We start stuffing it down. If you get good at your stillness, and you are listening, just watching the stream of consciousness, and as you are just watching it, you will hear these words. It is unbelievable that I cannot get this goal. I thought I was supposed to be better at _____ (whatever). I cannot believe myself. They are successful and a little pep talk occurs; It happens every day, multiple times a day. One out of ten we deal with, and the other nine we do not deal with, we stuff it down. That is a lot of wounding power going on, and it has got to go somewhere.

Sometimes we replay it; this is the key point to maxing out our "cup." If this starts happening, we are in trouble. So, the whole point of *S-S-S* is not necessarily just *creating our own goals* and creating our life from inside out, but it is also to check on what is going on inside. If we are at a specific place in our lives, there is always something, somewhere in there; otherwise, you would not be on the planet any longer. If we are already at this stage of replaying wounds over and over, we are there. We are maxed out. Parents often say, "I have had it up to here with you?" They have had it up to there (usually pointing at their forehead). They did not even know what they were saying. Their body is maxed out. It was not you specifically. You were just the little fizzle on top that made it all explode because everything underneath was finally pressuring up. The boiling water, if you will. So, become very aware of what is going on inside. Your center is shining, if, however, the system and the container surrounding it are **cloudy** then the shine is dull, and the internal state of affairs is in discord, which shows externally without the choice of where and when it shows and to whom.

Everyone is experiencing: You are not alone. We have had a few friends that felt the same. Millions of us that are going through that same experience, to a lesser degree perhaps, or more degrees, but it is the same concept. It shows up externally. Then when it comes to our business, whatever fear, doubt, worry, or concern that is still stuffed down about that topic that shows up. What do we do with that rejection? Nine out of ten, what do we do with it? That's called "*kick-the-cat syndrome.*" We start with the person closest to us. We will start with a co-worker. We will start venting. _____ Business is awfull and they are doing _____. Then you go to the next person. You work your way down the line. Then you go home, and you dump on your partner just because they are conveniently available and because, they are your partner and the day didn't go, as you desired. They are supposed to take the heat for you because you are having major malfunction, emotionally.

Continued example: Then if it is not good there with your partner, if you have kids, you yell at them to clean up their room! From there, the kid gets mad, and the kid goes down, finds a cat, kicks the cat that goes over and kicks the mouse. It starts all over again the next day, but nothing was ever solved, except the mouse keeps hiding! That is all that happens. We keep going through this cycle all the time. The state of affairs is in discord. When I first work with an athlete that is the first thing I look for, and I will ask three or four questions. I can figure out real fast, whether they are in peace, or they are in discord. Ninety-nine percent of the time, nine out of ten, they have nothing to do with peace. It is all *discord*. They are so lost in the distractions; their expectations; what they thought they would have or should be doing, that it starts to show up on their performance. Then that pressure externalizes itself, because now whatever field they are in, they will talk about them, as you are not playing well. You are a professional athlete. You have got to step up to your game." The pressure starts and now the "*kick-the-cat syndrome*" starts before you know it.

Of course, they were never in stress in the first place, which is the great illusion. Thus, the unconscious, seeking to protect the body that houses it, will *vent* internally until it reaches external boiling points. The subconscious has a vested interest in the body. Here "vent" means: Our stream of consciousness will start to change. We will start to hear those thoughts more often because it is trying to get them out; with *trying* being the operative word here because we are not letting it out and we just keep recycling it. They get stronger, and the voices get louder. The bills are starting to not get paid. We are not doing well at business. We cannot believe it. The family is starting to feel it and again the cat and mouse are both hiding now!

If left unexplored, this information will go inside, and you will not feel the difference in your life. This is the turning point right here. This is where you go back to your defined, predictable nine out of ten times. If left unexplored and unexpressed over time the effects are destructive for more "darkness" rules the internal and external experiences of the human. We start to go inside. We become very jaded, emotionally removed and repressed. We will not engage with anybody. No matter what opportunity comes, we find a way to screw it up, and we make it somebody else's fault. We blame them for it, which exacerbates the cycle.

Example from a movie: Recall the movie *Into the Wild*, which was done for different reasons, but it is a similar concept. It is a precursor to a nervous breakdown or an anxiety attack if you have ever had one of those. It is where you feel like you are just going to snap. It is awesome, the power that comes out of it. Imagine what they could be if they let the *Light* shine and turned it on, versus turned it off. This is the ultimate extreme. Let's agree that all of us have a power apart from this, at all times. No matter how clear we are. No matter how bright our *Light* is. Thus, it is our responsibility to look into the *abyss* of ourselves and clear out the emotions that are being *contained* within so they do not *vent* on our peace and other's peace. Let's be honest for a second. On an unconscious level, how many tried to steal your peace this week and what caused those actions from them?

- _____
  _____
- _____
  _____

Soggy potato chip theory

All we are doing is fighting over crumbs. There is a thing called the soggy potato chip theory. If you have watched our show (now off the air), we talked about it all the time. In relationships, it goes like this, and women are guiltier of this than men (although, men do it too). Women, you tend to go for soggy potato chips, because men are less well developed more often than women in general. Let's just agree with that and have an **example** of the soggy potato chip theory: If you find a starving man, and he has been starving, emaciated, and dehydrated, and you walk up to him and he asks for some food, but we offer a wet, soggy, moldy potato chip. What will the starving man do? Not only will he eat it, but he will also cherish it. "Thank you very much, you saved my life. Do you have another?" He does not care if it is moldy. He does not care if it is wet. He does not care if it looks like it has been out in the rain for 100 years, he will keep eating it. He will think it is wonderful because at least he is not starving, until someone comes along one day and offers him a dry, golden, lightly salted Ritz Cracker[3]. The moment he eats the Ritz Cracker, all of a sudden, the light bulb goes off that he was settling for a wet, soggy potato chip and did not know it. Now, in relationships, women you tend to settle for a lot of wet, soggy potato chips. We have done it too. All of a sudden you end up with somebody. Not that the person is bad every time, you just know that the energy is just not right, maybe you should not be there. This is a wet, soggy potato chip. Then you don't want to clean up all that wonderful emotion and what happens when you come around to someone next? "Well, I do not want to settle for a soggy potato chip so that I will settle for another kind of soggy potato chip." It is still a soggy potato chip. We just fooled ourselves, and we repeat the cycle. We do this with everything, not just relationships. We do this with our business. We keep choosing the same people expecting them to give a different answer. It is the definition of *insanity*, but the world needs more insane people than it needs sane people. Yet, this is not the insanity we speak of. We speak of, "Why are we drawing this cycle to us?" Let's look into the abyss, because when the abyss looks back, it does not have an emotional response. It does not care that it scares you. It just... is. So if you are scared on the inside, you are going to feel scared at most experiences subconsciously, and the abyss is going to look back when you dive into it and reflect your deepest fear.

There is an old saying that says, *"When a man looks into the abyss, and the abyss looks back, the character of the man is revealed."*

---

[3] Ritz Crackers are a brand of snack cracker introduced by Nabisco in 1934

The illusion is people find out who they are, or at least whom they think they are and never look back at the abyss of them.

Brief discussion

This is the ***most important part*** and the toughest part of the first five sessions of *Architect In Training* because it forces us to clear out the baggage that we are carrying. Let's have an example of a woman with intimacy and weight; she cannot lose the weight because, she keeps doing the same "shtick." She goes right back to the issue that has never been dealt with. The _____ and the _____ and all the things she went through but no one wants to talk about that, including her and those around her. What would it take to look in here (Spirit) and solve the problem? She has done so much for so many others. What is stopping her from taking care of her? It is the same thing. She is no different. We are all the same. So, we are going to look into the abyss.

This chapter is all about "***Emotionality.***" It is the emotions of going inside and discovering what you have been carrying and not looking at because they are bubbling up all the time. We are just not aware of them. Now, the trick is that we are becoming aware of them; a stream of consciousness. You start to hear the voices and notice *MOGs* by watching the external responses from people. Isn't it interesting in our relationships, even our business ones, more often than not, one person carries the load, and the other person gets dragged along. All the emotion comes out, and it blows this person up. The relationship destroys itself. Maybe you have had it happen already. Maybe you have had it in your personal lives. If you have not, it will eventually happen. Hopefully, you will get around it by doing this step, before it happens.

Coaching – Week Four

The first three emotions that show up and are not manufactured thoughts is our focus for now. These are our emotions that come up that are contained within. These are not manufactured. Like stacking, it is part of the manufacturer of our imagination. We are creating the experience before it happens and sticking it in the auto-code. This one, it is the reverse. You are going to go inside. We are going to show you the process later before you ask. This is what the introduction goals are: The first three emotions that come up, for some people, this will come just like that. Anger, guilt, frustration, resentment, or whatever it is. That is the first thing. There is more than three. I am just starting it simple.

Question is: Are you willing to let go of the emotions that you stuffed in your container? This sounds simple; but, when you are faced with the moment of choice, of willing to finally let yourself be free and be peaceful or stay in your confined moment and stay angry and stay upset and stay frustrated, more people will bail right here. We have already had people in this group bail from this five-week process and this scared the daylights out of them. It is not personal, but it will happen again. It will repeat its cycle. As it repeats itself, you will start to see it. Now, you can choose whether you want to participate or not. Questions to ponder:

- What are we doing?
- Are we stuffing this backdown?

We already know it is already easier, nine times out of ten, we know what we are going to get. The question is: Is that what we really want? Do you have to settle for that? Do you really have to settle for anything?

If you do, you must own the responsibility of your choice. It does not feel good, but you must own that. It is nobody else's choice, even in the married relationships and partnerships. The ultimate truth is that you are still only 50 percent of any relationship. It is challenging because sometimes you wish you were the whole 100 percent, don't you? We know, based on predictability, using the car example, nine out of ten times, we know what is going to happen. Therefore, I can feed my need to control, because at least I know if I am controlling it, it is better to reign in hell than it is to serve heaven. We do not know what is going to happen. We have just got to follow the *MOGs*. That leaves us a little out of control.

We have all bought into the illusion; no one is exempt from it and we have to go through this. Now, if you start adding to it, "one and two", you change the stacking of it, it is going to alter how your brain is going to perceive it. We also discussed about being a cheerleader and if you are not your own cheerleader, why is anybody else going to cheer for you?

Question to ponder:
What defines your success?

The question above is about making you look into the abyss now. It measures success differently than before, I used to have that external goal, but I discovered an ultimate truth for me. I invited you to look at that opportunity. I said after this week you could go back and be whatever you want. You can forget you even know me. It will be hard, but you can *try* it. *Don't* forget to remember me! The truth is, if you look at it from the ultimate truth, the thing that you were attached to be temporal, and that is the lesson that you are still learning. The question is: Are you going to let yourself learn it, this time? You are still you and wiser, no matter what happens from here, that is the good news. Now, whether you apply that wisdom remains to be seen, but you are carrying some baggage with it and how does that serve you to continue carrying it, besides being definable and predictable?

There are few elements added to that, because we were successful before we had these emotional structures. Now, they have exacerbated themselves, and we added a few friends, and you are keeping them. The success is not measuring via a litmus test comparing you to what you thought you were. It is psychological pain and time. People are still dealing with home issues, which we never dealt with in the first place, whatever they may be. They may be life-long. It is the external focus. I am driving you. If you notice the **common theme** here is: It is *inside out*, not outside in. That will be a great journey to discover who the heck you really are, not whom you think you are. We're running out of time, what are we waiting for? It is a choice, perhaps the greatest choice we will make in this lifetime.

What stop us from finally trusting ourselves? Perhaps the reason is that we have not met ourselves yet. You have met you from a manufactured point of view that you have created, which is called a "fracture." A fracture point from trauma, mom/dad/religion/state etc., probably created it. "You have got to be this way. You have got to work hard. You have got to take care of yourself. You have got to be tougher because, man, it is tough out there. It is tough in the real world. People will screw you over. You have all this stuff still playing in your head from when you were a child that just comes right out of you. Let's flip the script. When will you stop being so emotionally driven about having to do everything for those who "programmed" you? Are you using your anger to feel more powerful as means of dealing/not dealing with those drivers in your mind? It does not make us the bad person because we are all angry at something, sometime in our lives.

The problem is that there is a **stereotypical myth** that says, "If you say anything bad about somebody, you are a bad person yourself." Maybe your mom caused psychological pain because you did not know what you did not know when you were young. You are just a computer sucking up what mom and dad say, all day long. They are flawed creatures too, but you have to make peace with it, that is where the disconnect remains.

Emotionality: The only difference is you did not put in peace first, and that is exactly why you must go to peace first and let it bubble up. Because if we do not we get lost in the emotion again. It takes us over because there is so much stuff bubbling up. All of a sudden, you are like, "Gibberish," throwing up. We all do it. Most of the people did it. The reason others react, is that you touched sore spots on them. They are saying, "I have got issues just like that too." We all find out that we are all messed up, together. Most people are uncomfortable with that because they have not even gotten to stillness yet. They are still running around, running on the programs saying:

- I have got to go to an Ivy League School.
- I have got to make millions of dollars.
- I have got to marry the right person.
- I have got to birth out three kids.
- I have got to do all this stuff.

Mom/Dad, do you approve of me? You are left with this dumbfounded look. Let's extrapolate this. My fantasy is that you have built this very successful life to prove to mom/dad how awesome you were, and no one has ever done this. All of a sudden you got to that point, and there is this *pseudo-epiphany* that came along where you start to realize that no matter what you did, it was not going to matter. So, subconsciously, you tore it all down, and you started destroying it, because at that point you had worked, all of your efforts, for nothing. "Effort" is the key word.

Now, the point is we have this opportunity to finally live our life for us, look into the abyss. You just looked at it, and it looked right back. The funny thing is that we are more connected to ourselves now than before exploring internally, because now we can feel ourselves. It does not mean you have to be like this all the time, although it is hard to be that way as well. As you let those come out, more of us comes out and we cheer about it. The effort does not become so hard. Now you have put forth effort for a different reason. We are putting forth effort for peace and calm and being who we want to be. We do not trust ourselves to travel yet, because we have not quite gotten to know ourselves yet, because we have been so busy doing it for mom or for husband or for our kid or whatever. I think that is a *MOG*, by the way. Our success or failure is not based on the outside world, religion, State, or mom or dad; now it is just based on our real selves, coming from Spirit and without all the emotional baggage being carried along. That is freedom.

CHAPTER 7

Architecting360 Training V

(Placing thoughts in motion)

Introduction:

In the last chapter, if you take one and two and go beyond that session, what you do is you start labeling the "spaces." For example, the two moves over and three is up, just like you did with the one and two to create the "space" for your mind to rest. Now the "topic" is about **M-O-N-E-Y,** instead of just seeking space between your thoughts. Everyone has a money goal, some of you really want to accomplish this and so now, you stare at "nothing" as you come back and "stack" (step three) in that topic. The three moves over and four comes up. Now we have another topic. The top ten things are the most important things and we should work our way through those with great diligence and care. We are discussing it only because there are "measurable" litmus tests to show in these particular training sessions, how we tend not to make our goals happen. Some of us work on outcomes. They want their brain constantly doing different things, searching, evolving, and pulling more stuff up. For example, when we look at the *Tacoma Dome*, it is just one of them and, yet again, when you get into different versions of, it called "*subconscious* *spontaneity*" other ideas, directions, goals and outcomes can and often do arise. When we step back from an outcome, and look at something that is that big, then we leave room for the subconscious *Spirit* to move on things that we had not thought of and not limit ourselves. That may be the way we want it to go, but then we miss all of the stuff on the outside of the box because we put ourselves into one. In this way we are opening up to a larger outcome just like the Tacoma Dome.

At the end of this chapter, we will know how to find ourselves in the questions, as our minds have morphed beyond what it originally was and because the other things are now, less than important from when we started this journey. Now it is really what we want it to become.

Questions to Ponder:

1. Stillness:

- Did you do your stillness?
- How was it this session?
- What did you discover about your conscious mind? How long in "Time" did you stay in stillness?
- What prevented you from going inside?

2. Spacing:

- How many times this week did you practice spacing?
- What was longest, you held space between your thoughts?
- How many times did you have to "start over?"
- How long before you finally stopped due to having to start over?

3. Stacking:

- What did you discover about placing what you want into your auto code?
- How long did you stare at your vision?
- Did you wander off your vision?
- Were there any patterns in that wandering?

4. Emotionality:

- What emotions bubbled up most dominantly?

This is going back to that example from last session; it feels like a lifetime, surely. Time is distorted when you are having fun. The most dominant example, in most cases, would be that "I/we are not good enough."

These questions are written frequently, to explore the further.

If we make at least one "root" realization and release it, that will be fair enough. In most cases, we made the realization from the last chapters work, assuming you did the step. The question is how does that change our life experience and how did it change us? What kept you from reaching the *root* in your case?

Subconscious Speaks: There was a great study many, many years ago (It was about 15 years ago now.), down in Australia, which was called *Reverse Speech.* What they would do is they would take a stream of consciousness thought, where someone was just talking about something randomly, and they would replay it backward, and you would hear a word forward from the unconscious relating to that topic. It is phenomenal. It was an excellent experiment. It really was, they went all they went all the way back to J.F.K. assignation and O.J. Simpson trial. We brought it over here and did it in some experimenting with it. It was interesting to hear how people would say what they were really thinking subconsciously. It was a just stream of consciousness; because, with our stream of consciousness, the unconscious is speaking it all the time, which is why when you meet somebody you feel connected with right away or vice versa via disconnection. You have those experiences, and you say, "Deja vu." It is always speaking.

Goals for Week Four

It's time to decide what were our goals for this session and how many did we achieve? What stopped us from achieving all of them? Where have we heard that before? So, again, we are going to float through that so this will go a little faster.

Now, based on what we have done through this session, on our microcosmic version, what is this feeling about loyalty issue that we are struggling with. People do it, but they do it with an attitude, or they do it in their own way. We fight here to discover who we are and our choices and what were the anger points about with this, because what we were discussing. There is a changed question, "*Why* did I have the reaction versus what did I feel and where did it come from?" We just did emotionality, dive into it. We felt an intense loyalty with that person, correct? Was that a real or a superficial reaction? What emotion did we feel underneath that?

There is the defense mechanism that needs your attention. That says, "I do not know." How does it serve us to keep all that stuff down _____?

That is what we have been dealing with for the last six chapters. So what if you "Explode" your mind, and let it all out? This is a feeling response. This is personal coaching time. Lighten up a little bit, and allow yourself to feel your feelings. Was it nervousness, anxiousness, anticipation, excitement, or fear?

It is probably in anticipation of discovering whom you are when that fear comes up. Nine times out of ten, often, fear will disguise itself as anxiety. Anticipation will usually hide in fear because we do not want to get excited about really letting ourselves out because the ego has a say and you could be freer. So, it will put fear into it and give it a mask. The "mask" as meaning the hiding something, root within via an external "face" or representation to the external world. How can we stick up for somebody else if we have yet to do so for ourselves? It is not about sticking up for other people. Some people need to be spoken up for. We are speaking up for people who are not speaking up to get them to where they need to be, right.

Question to ponder: "When/Where do you stand up for you?"

The challenge is: This is my rough read on us from a, Psych 101 point of view, from a distance. Some people have a very large heart, very compassionate, some are a very emotional and some are compressed, which is why the "flat lined" example about passing through life, resonated with compressed readers, from a certain point of view. Correction, it was more of a trampling and stuffing down of our *Spirit*, numbing down the emotions. In that case we are not allowed to speak our true mind. Now, we have a way to read the mind and say, "Well, no, this is what that person was saying. See, I can speak my mind about them, but I still cannot do it for me." Final thought on this point, we can't teach what we do not know ourselves. Thus, start internally with you, find the root of your compression, then express it, live it, be it and guide others.

Placing Thought in Motion

There is no other option, and luxury of thoughts that lead us from a state of *no* peace, is over. Remember peace or no peace. From this point forward, you can no longer afford the luxury of it because you now know what it will do, and we are responsible for its doing now. Therefore, if you continue with the line of thought that says, "I am going to fight for them and I am not going to fight for myself," it transforms itself and becomes a very, very strong thing. Now the question, in the most simplistic of versions, is now you can identify when we are doing our stillness and spacing:

- Does this thought invite me to peace or no peace?
- Does this person offer to peace or no peace?

All we need do is feel it. It's not about being judgmental. It means that you feel the response and know where to go. You feel the emotional response, and you go. Do I feel peaceful about it or do I not? If you do not know, what do you do? Stop, get still, go inside, and bring it up until you do know one way or the other. What I am saying is, if a person comes into your experience, giving you the feeling of discord and no peace and you think he is a bad person (judgment). Opposed to saying, at the moment, there is no peace about it (non-judgment). You are taking responsibility for yourself. You are not going to change them. That is not the objective because you cannot do that, but you watch how you respond. The truth is maybe you are judging, hence, why you are feeling no peace, (We are getting ahead of ourselves.), but you started watching the thought process. Now, we know:

- What the "thoughts" do in our heads.
- What *stream of consciousness* is,
- How to interrupt it,
- What it does from a programming point of view.
- We know how the *Spirit* is going to help us manifest it.

We are ultimately judging how we are responding; and, if we are getting in a state of no peace, maybe that particular person is rubbing us in the wrong way. It is our responsibility to take responsibility for ourselves and choose to butt heads with this person, or we can go, we know it's not about peace. Then, it is not about anyone else. It is about us. So keep the peace. If you come back, and you still run into it again, maybe you do not need to be there. If you let your peace go, (We have already talked about this at the beginning of last session if you will.), they will take it, because it is a lot easier to take our peace instead of keeping it. It is easier to stay at peace or to steal someone else's peace? That is why there are *energy vampires*. It is easier to steal them from us, because we do all the work, and is probably what people have done to you, or perhaps you have done it to another.

Now, how to interpret that? Is that *peace* or *no peace*? Let's have an example of a picture of woman meditating. If you pre-judge it, you are a part of the problem. We have no idea if she is in peace or not, we don't have enough interaction with her, as it is just a picture example for our exercise here. She is actually in a peaceful state. She was just calm in a stony-state of meditation. I am in contemplation and deep thought. Therefore, this one is actually in peace. If you look at her eyes, they are not wrinkled; her forehead is not browned; and there is nothing here. She is just calm, but she chooses to do meditate in this way. It was just a great thing. When we found this picture, it seems that its presentation messes people up, and that is the point. Now, all of a sudden, we have discord due to our pre-judging, accidentally, but the possibly is there she maybe. On the other hand, she is really in peace.

We are our thoughts, and thoughts are things that become real either internal or external. Therefore, the option and luxury to continue thinking the thoughts that drive you to a state of no peace will become real internal and external. Therefore, we are now responsible for our lives from this moment on. In whatever you do, if I never see you again, and I hope that is not truth, but if that becomes a reality, you will forever be affected by this truth. What you do with it is up to you, period. You own your own life, it's called *FREEDOM*. It scares the daylights out of a lot of people. Take an example of a soap opera: Most of people have never even watched one. Have you watched a soap opera? If *yes* what is the number one thing about soap opera? They repeat themselves. Therefore, if you checked out 30 years ago and you come back in you will know the storyline in 2 minutes. The news is pretty much the same way and we can't fix them.

We can check in with our Spirit/gut, just like the thoughts in our head, you can watch the object go by on the screen, but you do not have to participate. If you get a reaction to it, step back and weigh the emotionality. Therefore, we watch how it brings up the things in us that is all we can really control and do in this lifetime. This is called the *dragon state*. Do you study martial arts or you ever heard of Bruce Lee?

His nickname was the *Dragon*. Did you know why he is called: "The Dragon?" (As we discussed in session one), are these mythical creatures that have always been around. Sometimes, they are feared, sometimes they are majestic, they can fly away, they have scales of wisdom, and they can blow fire. They can do all of these mythical things. The thing about a dragon is the dragon has all of the ability to fight and survive but has the wisdom to know when to do it. A tiger, which is one notch below, is always reactionary and always destructive. A tiger kills when it responds. A dragon will kill, if you keep going. Otherwise, it is going to fly away and wait for another day: but, if we keep coming, we are done for and it has the wisdom to carry it out. Tigers do not have wisdom, just raw power and reaction; kind of like most humans wouldn't you say?

MOG: We talked about the tiger versus the dragon. At this point, I call it *The Dragon;* because, at this point, you have the knowledge and the wisdom, but how you employ it will make you a tiger or dragon. If you are being a "tiger" it means you are a reactive person. You are out there just throwing stuff and you do not even realize that you are doing it. Alternatively, you are going to stop finally and differentiate between peace and no peace. *Example*: Bruce[4] was a dragon mind, body, and spirit. His work is still affecting

---

[4] Bruce Lee was a famous Hong Kong American martial artist, action film actor, martial arts instructor, philosopher, filmmaker, and the founder of Jeet Kune Do.

people, long after his body has left the building. His philosophies are phenomenally eternal, not only in the martial arts world but also in cinematography and movies and writings. I mean, if you have ever watched *The Bruce Lee Story*, it is impressive stuff. It's a blessing that one of my experiences was with Sifu Dan Inosanto who was Bruce Lee's student and training partner. So, I had some teachings from him and this is something that is obviously important to me, but that is why I named this level *Dragon*.

At this point, whether you go another step further in this process or not, you now know enough to be a dragon. You know 95% more of the people out there in the United States, perhaps the world, how mentality works. So, you can be a dragon that breathes fire. There are black dragons, which are ones that are to be feared. There are red dragons, which are masters; they have learned, "I am responsible for me. I can manifest this if I want to. I can change myself, which ultimately changes the world." So, we call it *Dragon*.

Its actual function is called: **Thought-In** and **Thought-Out**, but I call it *Dragon* from this right here (Spirit/gut), the luxury of thoughts, *luxury*. Readers this, experiencial tool, is a luxury. I know and you can now attest to that as well. A newborn baby does not have this luxury, yet!

Everybody already is one whether they are a golden, black, red, or green dragon. I do not care what color. There are green dragons too. Be a purple one. It's nothing about what color you want to be. We just call it *Dragon;* because, if I ask someone, "Are you in *Dragon (Spirit)* right now," and they respond, then I know they have been through our process in some form or another, and they understand what I am talking about.

Dragon and Tiger: From this moment on we must assume full responsibility for our thoughts, choice, and life, hence *Dragon*. *Dragon* implies mastership. Tiger implies almost a master, has the knowledge, but not the wisdom to employ its knowledge with guided and directed preciseness. A dragon can go and just knock it out, but a tiger kills everything. A killing tiger is brutal, and it is very powerful and very reactive. Sometimes in emotionality, we are tigers. You just destroying everything, are we not? Dragons do not, very persistent. You are very responsible for yourself. So I call it *Dragon*.

A daily and moment-to-moment awakened state must be kept, as this is the "trick" of a dragon, *Thought-in/Thought-Out*, being aware of it at all times. When we started from first session, it was challenging, some four now/five sessions ago theoretically, that stillness was hard. We are doing 10-to-15 minutes a day now with no problem. So is it possible that this is possible? We have to find out, what makes it impossible inside us. **Nothing, it is not impossible**. It is whether you want to do it. You may not and that is okay. Some people like being tigers; they enjoy the power, raw power, of being a tiger until they meet a dragon. Then, they have a problem.

The subconscious programs are continually monitored and upgraded as we change; this is why it is asked: "How are you different now from session four." We have been monitoring our programs in stillness, in stacking, and in spacing. We are watching the stream of consciousness. We are watching our daily interactions. We are watching them while having a conversation, but now we are responding to them, or we walk into space, and we do not feel comfortable. Up until this moment of our life, how often have we been distracted and we been not even aware of what we were doing. The responses from the conscious mind are something like:

- What else better do you have to do?
- I have to get this done?
- This is what I do every day.

Wherever you go, there you are and you are not getting out of your skin. Some people have a response, that it is habitual. Do you ever get tired of hearing someone say the same thing? But, if we watch the stream of consciousness, we will start to see the habits we are being driven by at the subconscious level. Then decide whether we want to change them or not. If not, then we have to own it. If it brings a result that we do not want, we are going to look at ourselves. Look back at the abyss inside you, again.

Spirit: If allowed to, the conscious mind will wander all over this Universe. Go back to session One; anatomically it is built that way. It is a defense mechanism. It only guards one wall in your mind's "castle". That means three "walls" are always exposed, which allows, desired or not, new and unwanted programs to invade your subconscious computer and will invent more "habits" that mess us up. Suppose by now, you thought you cleared something out, and then you have something else to deal with, right. I am sure we have done it in this five-session process alone, imagine what has gone on your life before know what you know now. Recall always, we are a spiritual being having a human experience. Until that part of your, *Spirit* leaves your body, there will always be something to deal with, change, upgrade or delete from within. It is an inevitable fact. Since the conscious mind is built that way, it is only going to filter so much before something gets by its "guard". So, by becoming aware of it, at least, we reduce the possibility of adding more "stuff" that we did not want, but there is always already "stuff" that we did not want anyway. We are always going to have something to deal with. The journey is this, (I totally understand where you are going with this, and I agree with you), the excitement of going forward and not to participate in an old habit, because we can even leave the "Stuff" on the road and let someone else step in it since we seem to be on a "Stuff" theme. This has gone from "Discussions with your Inner Psychologist" to, The Street Gutter Psychologist version.

State of manic: The state of manic, the state of absolute insanity or the nervous breakdown. We can interpret it all of those different ways, and this one is that way. It is designed that way to show that we will continue to repeat the habits. It is cyclical. Using this one as a counter is a cyclical effect that works to the cyclical thing that we naturally do to undo it, and ultimately get more of our *Light* to shine. This potentially brings us to a state of internal and external disruption or a no-peace state. Thus, we must watch our thoughts constantly. You have to watch the watcher constantly, for he too is still a subconscious program. Questions to ponder:

- Where are we "watching" from?
- Where does stillness come from?

We are watching from *Spirit*. The solar plexus area is watching from inside, watching the thoughts, and watching the external reactions to yourself: Yet, still experiencing your life. Too many people when they go to meditate, and maybe you experienced this when you started, they step so far back that they experience nothing. They flat line, not to bring that back up, but let's bring it up. It's just an observing, processing and watching the reactions. For the love of God, pull the stop cork out of that drain and let's roll. It does not mean that we cannot experience life!

The unchecked brain, (not mind, brain), left on its own leads us to a path of discord and distractions. Therefore, we must change our thoughts. Go back to stillness to do that. Start with observation. We start looking at the "spacing" so that we can create a "gap" in the conscious stream of random thoughts. This time, they will be larger gaps. Soon they will become nice, big, chunky gaps. Then you will have gaps where there is just nothing there, and you can just enjoy peace. That will be a nice state of mind. You probably will be experiencing this as we go through stacking, through emotionality, and as we come back around.

Five steps: To change our thoughts, we simply follow the five steps. We have all done it now. It is not as if you have to go experience anymore. To allow our internal spirit to bridge us to out external world, thought by thought, *MOG* by *MOG*. Have you ever noticed as *MOG's* started coming and you first experienced *MOGs* and went through this, they start to get a little more frequent. You start to notice them a little more and the more you notice something, the more "it" shows up, the more they happen, and all of a sudden, you just have to follow the *MOGs*. It is almost like following the crumbs to the gingerbread house; it is a similar concept.

The bridge I want to talk about is not specifically in the five sessions, but we are going to throw it anyways. The *bridge* is a psychological word based on, psychodynamics. We agree that thoughts are things. Let's say we get stuck in a *negative loop*. We cannot get the stillness. We cannot get the spacing. It is just one of those days where everything that could go wrong did. You had this thought that keeps repeating, and It is thought that you do not want. How do you get out of it? It is called a "*bridge*", which is the word "And" is here and there is always a *bridge* out of a conversation, stream of conscious thoughts and our internal habits. There is always a way to change our thoughts. Let's have an examples of kids: If you have children or have ever been around a child, you will understand this; a little one walks up to you and he/she is pulling on your sleeve, and you are trying to have a conversation, and he/she keeps pulling, and you ignore the child, what does the child do? He/She gets louder and goes from being on the side of you until he gets right in front of your face of you until you bark loudly at him, with a "WHAT!"

Now, what ends up happening, just like that child, the *negative thoughts* in our head are going to clamor constantly for our attention, all of them. It is going to keep working its way until its right in front of us. Boom and that is all we see, and you cannot get around it. The reason being is if we do not acknowledge the voice, it cannot shut up because it is a part of us. You do not have to participate with it to achieve acknowledgment. Too many times we get lost in the thought itself and Its "blabbering" and then you dive into it, "blabbering," and then you get lost in it. Now, all of a sudden, we are in the *negative spiral*. Our "bridge" is the way out to where we want to go, and you may have to do these three, four, or five times. If you do it, you will eventually "cross the bridge" out the cloudiness, and that other thought that you want will show up. We use it in professional sports all the time because the conscious mind will throw "stuff" at you randomly; like "we cannot do it" and we have to get that out of my mindset quickly and also got to concentrate. It keeps coming back, "You cannot do it." Maybe when you have been doing a business presentation, you may have a voice in your head that says, "They are not getting it. They are not going to buy this?" What you normally do is try to ignore it and is generally doesn't go well. By using "and" you can simply acknowledge the thought followed by "and now I/we are going to believe they are getting it" and redirect your internal thought energy. Does this mean every time you bridge out it will always go your way, no but, assuredly if you do not bridge out you will be repeating processes over and over again for sure, as you have already seen here.

The flat line: What is the matter if someone calls you nuts? They do not know why they called you nuts, but they will pick up that there is something going on inside you. There is a conflict on the inside and simply saying, "They may not be getting it, and now I am going to focus on giving them the invitation." What happens is this thought will dissipate. Now, you can't agree with the original thought because if you agree with it, it now becomes a reality check. That means they are not getting it, which means now it is going to become real because now there is energy is it. Psychologically, we can direct our thoughts where we want them to go. That is what bridge out means. That is a dragon. A tiger gets lost in the fight, and inside there is a war.

We are more than we "think" we are unless we "think" we are less. Here the word *think* is in quotes for a reason. It has nothing to do with what you think. Your brain is going stay here inside your skull, but your thought process can make you something/anything, and perhaps it has already happened to you. It's not that it's who we are, but it is whom we act like and whom you think you could have been. You will experience that all the way to the nines. You did everything and still did not get what you wanted. This is what concerns me personally, which is why I do not watch the news for example. If you want to see what stillness looks like and spacing looks like, stacking, watch a the newscast. "Now today, someone got shot; a car ran over someone; someone got killed; 400 million people blew up; by the way, oil prices are going up; and the sky is falling. Don't forget the stock market sucks, but please invest your money." On and on and on if you stare at it long enough, you are de-facto doing "one and two." You are just staring at the hypnotic TV in the middle and presto; you are stacking into your subconscious! Why do you think people are scared to death, literally, in the world right now and where did the money go? We invented it. It is a tangible thing. It is energy. The banks are all still here, readers. Most of us bank every day just like we do. The money is still there. The question is:

- Where did it go?
- Where did the energy change?

Well, you know why, they put a mindless state of fear out there, and people bought it. They bought it. Is oil really, necessarily getting to be $120.00 a barrel versus $60.00?

They did it because they pushed our boundary all the way up to $5.00 for a gallon of gas; and, now, $3.00 becomes acceptable. It is a better bargain than $5.00, right. We bought it because we tuned in to the "thought process." The news week to week is almost identical. Somebody was killed; somebody blew up; we are still in war; oil prices are going up; the stock market sucks. By the way, the whole real estate thing is terrible. Everything sucks. The economy is going to be great in three years.

How do they know the economy is going to be great in three years? "They" are creating it for us. It is a freaking mindset. Now you watch, two years from now, we will be back. Houses will be on the market, high as ever. Everyone is going to be back in debt again. It is just a cycle, people. The question is: *"Are we going to participate in it?*" Some people think that we are making this all a conspiracy theory, but no; just watch the cycles of history. It is not rocket science. We already discussed that most fortunes are made in down cycles by those who are not of that mindset, stay awake and look for your *MOGs, the ones you created inside now appearing in the outside.* They are always there. People always see *MOGs* when they feel euphoric and safe. "We have $10,000.00 in the bank, and our stocks are doing well. Our 401(k) is finally a 401(k)." Everything is right in the world commonly known as a *Comfort zone.* As soon as that comfort zone gets threatened, they are in trouble.

Part of what life brings is an interesting opportunity is to wake people up. It keeps challenging you to define YOUR story and tell your story the way you want it to be, literally. Your story should be awesome, especially since it's your own, if we walk down the street, (Let's agree that the desert (Palm Springs) is dead right now. We are not in high visitor season. There are still people here ironically, but we will call it "dead", not that it wasn't great anyways, for whatever strange, odd reason, because without people we get scared), with a camera right now, and we went down there, and you just acted like you were interviewing and we just playing crew for you and you interview people, about being concerned about their retirement. I bet you get 10 out of 10 agreements, if you asked if they ever lost money in the stock market. Do you think you can get 10 people to listen to an investment opportunity after getting them in that state of mind of how do I safely grow my money? It is a no-brainer. Tell your story and invite others into your story.

Revolution: In Architect of BEing™, we called it *The Revolution.* In one of shows, we talked about the revolutions of old; the days of those are gone. The days of those who can **and** teach are here. Teach them, because you have already built a plan/life/business/ relationship so you know how to do it. What is that worth in dollars and cents and knowledge? How many zeros do you want, because the person who had never got to where you were before you "lost it"? You are already a dragon to them. They are still lost. They are not even tigers yet. Now, you can take the energy of the dragon, and ignite people. It also clears out all that "stuff", so you can realize that we got in bed with someone who did not take care of us. This time, we have to take care of ourselves and it is a little bit selfish. But; if you are not, someone might steal your *Light*. I do not mean to be paranoid, but, again, it is easier to take your money than it is for me to make it with you.

Here is a question: "What are the most dominant thoughts that keep repeating in your brain? Peace or no peace. That is all we need. Make it the most dominant one. If there are dominant thoughts that move you to no peace, then go back and discover where there is no peace. The emotional current is coming from somewhere inside your body-your calves or arms, for example. They are coming from somewhere or your chest, perhaps. You feel that for clamp of tightness from time to time and yet it is still our body. The funny thing is, there is no rhyme or reason for where it will stick. You might think, you broke a rib but you feel the emotion down somewhere. It is where it puts itself. In all of my training, I have asked every psychologist, every psychiatrist, and everyone I have ever met, and they do not know. *Spirit* is where it puts itself. Again, I tend not to get lost in the *how* I get into in the *what*.

Let's go to the example of "calves"; because, if I have you dive in your calves, that emotion will come right up for me. We can analyze it, or we can get on with it, whatever you want to do. This is the most dominant thought. That is awesome by the way. That right there is awesome. That is what we live for. That is what is important to us. Knowing that, so the difference between *thinking* and *knowing* and *tiger* versus *dragon*. The tiger will see if it works. If it does not, roar. The dragon moves over if it does not work and finds another way. Throw something at someone, and see how he or she responds and how you are responding at the same time. It is going to be an ultimate a game of psych connection or psych warfare. It is your choice. I prefer psych connection; although, I do play psych warfare from time to time. Is your first action when you identify these thoughts, to react to it (tiger), or do you or respond via your *Spirit*? So, again it's about *MOG*.

Questions to ponder:

- Did we have a choice?
- What did you choose to do with it?
- Did you get a response from your choice?
- Was it different from the choice you made prior to?
- Can you repeat the choice again?
- Can you make it bigger or more detailed?

That was easy, it is not lying or going high or low emotionally; you just are you. Even though it's tough enough, being you. Point to notice: When you identify these thoughts, how do you do that? It's already discussed. How do you do this process and how do you identify it? Go all the way back to the beginning. How do you identify a thought? What is that? What did I say about constantly watch your thoughts and identify them. So the first thing you do is always go back to that. This is the first thing right here (Spirit/ gut) when the dragon speaks, watch the thought. When you have a thought come into your mind, you have the choice to react to it, bridge out or respond differently to it. You can respond to these thoughts then you can change them to thoughts you want, couldn't you? We have all changed thoughts in here during this event and its process.

This is an embedded code by the way. There is a whole other language, which I call the "Magik 7". As we discussed there is a whole other language in psychodynamics. It's written just because I want, to be honest with you readers. I am programming you right now as you read this. It is hypnotic. It is an "if-then" sequence and there are several levels of how a person responds: negation through awareness and directness is just one of them. Anyways, if you read this, and you watch the way the statement is phrased, you can use negation, but you did not hear from me. It is called a "**subconscious agreement**." If someone show you a car and says if I can get it to you today, then would you buy it? Isn't that an if/then question? If you would agree with me that your 401(k) is probably not going to be anything more than a 101(k), then it is probably the truth that we need to take responsibility for our financial fortune, correct? Do you see how you can change that offer by using the "if-then"? It is the same thing. Now there is a whole other book/training by really diving into the "Magik 7" of human communication but this is just one little thing you can use to change how you speak to others and more interestingly with yourself.

There is nothing more else to do. Then, life becomes a people business, because they will open up, immediately. Have fun with that. If we respond to the thoughts, the positive ones, which means we can change anything we want, anytime we want. *Surrender, accept*, or whatever word fires for you.

Though-In/Thought-Out

Dragon – Is directing our thoughts towards true desires and internal peace.

This means that we are constantly aware of the thoughts that we are thinking; because, if we are not aware of it, and someone else throws a suggestion at us, whether they are aware of it or not, it can get by one of the "guards" of our conscious mind. It is a lot of fun, but we should do it in a way to open people up and give them the invitation, and they will respond. I do not want to fry your brain because psychodynamics will fry you, at first. *Thought-in/thought-out* - means thought inside, thought out not think this way or that way. It means coming from Spirit here out to the world. I think it inside, I feel it inside, and I thought it and I push it out into the world via speaking it, feeling it, the energy of it and identifying the MOGs.

Question:

Is directing our thoughts at all times towards what we want really from the internal *Spirit*?

By using stillness, spacing, stacking and thinking out of the thoughts that move us into no peace and distractions we are *Architecting* our lives. What I mean by "thinking out of" is being so aware of the thoughts that move us into no peace, that we can bring the bridge back out at any given time to bring back the thoughts of peace or experiences of peace or behaviors of peace, because we already have those, do you not? If not from this five weeks, but your life already, but now for sure you have them, after this experience. Now, you can totally change what this life is about for you. This is what happened to me. Most on my team have had the same experience. Now, we can drop the anger about it; or, we can then take that anger and turn it from a no-peace state to a peace state. There are people who have been there before. They have a look in their eye. So, when you have been there, you know that you know.

For obvious reasons, start in stillness, clear the mechanism, get calm and observe the thought process. Do spacing for one-to-three minutes, stacking for three-to-five minutes, and emotionality for five-to-ten minutes. Will this go longer than that that is up to you personally? Mathematically it is about 30 minutes a day. It hasn't to be all at once. There are no rules, do at a stoplight, as long as it is red and you know when you need to go. I am not condoning you drive with your eyes closed; although, it is possible. At that point you can read your mind; say get out of my head and bridge out to what you want. It is funny, really if you watch yourself. Observe your thoughts. Now, this becomes important because now is where the cyclical effect happens. We are now bringing this around where it becomes a nice turning machine, where you can start to drive your life, and I mean literally. Now you are observing your thoughts from this point of view (Spirit) but with this concept (Peace or No-Peace). Now you have done all this; now you start to observe your thoughts again. Then, you start to identify dominant thoughts. You start to identify thoughts that are drawing you from peace or no peace, and you can walk right through this process again, and you start going faster. You can go as fast as you want to go. Some people want to go slow; some people want to go fast. You can create this as fast as you want because now you are watching the thoughts and you are driving them. If you are not driving your mind, who is?

This is just observation, not rocket science. This is going to wake you up. Dragon is where you become awake; that is what is most loveable about this. If peace, fill your container with a *Light*. That is stacking. Let our *Light* shine. Session three, push it out and experience it. The more you push it out, the more it *MOGs* back to you. It is not rocket science. You can make it rocket science, but it is not. Now, those people that you presented your business to differently, how do all respond to you? The more you do it, the more they are going to come towards you. Because you have your spiritual gift, but the truth is what they are catching onto is that you are waking them up. To feel that funny feeling is a *MOG*, and maybe it is time for us all to wake up.

What is a MOG: Now, if you recall MOG is a Moment of Grace, but we will get back to that. Eventually, someone is going to ask you what a *MOG* is. When you explain a *MOG* to someone, it is a very magical moment when they say, "This person is talking about something totally different than what I thought they were talking about. I thought you were talking about network marketing pyramid schemes. You are talking about something totally different." If no peace, redirect to what we want. Bridge out, start over, walk through it, identify it, and work it all the way down. If that no peace thought is still there, dive right into it. Stop avoiding you. Look into the darkness of you, and bring the *Light*. Bring the emotionality out. Go back to more peace. The more peace, the quicker they come. We have to work on that to reprogram our minds to think only *thoughts of **want** and **peace***. Here *want* and *peace* meant by: "What do we want, and what keeps us in peace?" If you go in those two simultaneously:

- Is this what I want.
- Is this my peace?

If we constantly do that, where is all your energy going? To those things, and the more you are cleaning out, the more the *Light* shines, and it becomes cyclical in stacking and emotionality. Now, you are a dragon, because now you are responsible and own it. If we decide to take somebody out verbally, we have chosen it, hopefully you didn't, but it will probably happen. Life is life. We have more opportunities now not to take them out but to invite them out. Take their energy and tell them about *MOGs*. It is a totally different experience because now you are using it. You are controlling it. This is the control we all want, all talk about, but do not use.

Homework

You have never heard this before: **S-S-S, E** (This, again, is the slang way we say this.), and thought in/though-out three or four times a week. Thought-in/thought-out means that we are taking this to the level of Spirit/Dragon. It's about stacking at a harder level. Thought in/thought-out; we can no longer think thoughts that take us to no peace. Now, with all this in place, it will take us to peace.

Discover and document percentage wise: Which is more dominant, peace, or no peace? It is not because you want to give yourself a good butt kicking, but it is just to start to discover sixty percent of the time we are in peace. As we disscuss earlier nine out of ten times, there is a "no," but what if you gave yourself permission nine out of ten times a "yes?" They made a movie about it, in a kind of lame way, called, *"Yes Man"* with Jim Carey, where he had to say, "yes" to everything. Obviously, that is an extreme. That is not what I mean by saying, "Yes." What I mean is, "Listen to your *Spirit,* but give yourself the opportunity to say "yes" to peace, no matter what it is, even if it seems illogical, because *your body can not contain all light. Spirit* is too big for it. Otherwise, you would explain the universe. Sometimes you will be asked to do things in your *Spirit* that make no sense, like coming to this book and the workshop.

Corporate America has more of replicated structure than network marketing; although, corporate will tell us the opposite. They will not ask you to do as they do; you have just to do like they do or you are fired. Question to ponder:

- What does that mean to me internally?
- How do I just do it with peace?
- What does saying simply, "yes" to _____ create emotionally for me?

This is a real tough one right here, only because it is going to challenge you to the ultimate test of you. Go one day, then two days, where you are so in tune with the *Spirit* that you can direct any thought: No matter what is presented, to where you "want" and "peace." All day, not one thought do you let escape you. When you get to that space, you are a dragon. What will you do now, when everyone can honestly come back and there is a look in his or her eye that can be seen, this is when you become a dragon. I do not know how to explain it to you. I just know it. I can see it. I mean, "got it" as if you possess it fully. I mean, "Got it" as if you are experiencing your life now. This is the ultimate for you in the five-session to get to the space.

When you do this one-day, then it will become two, and then it will become three... It will become such a habit that you will just be talking to people left and right. People will walk to you, and they will *MOG* you out and then tell you that there is something different about you and you have a peace, knowingness and calmness. You will give him an invitation by sharing your experience and you invite them. Ultimately, at the end of the day, any way you slice it, you can call it money, sex, drugs, or rock and roll, whatever you want to call it, it is going to boil down to that. That was part of what retirement was about, "The freedom to choose where and when my time is used". Even retirement has its drawbacks because then you have to invent things to do. So, from this point of view, you are inventing whole other levels of things to do.

It doesn't that have anything to do with the business presentation, although it does. We believe rules are for people who cannot make their own decisions. Society governs itself. We do not need all the laws, especially if you are doing this. If you get a hold of this, which everybody can do, it is just whether they are willing to do it. It is just a process of going through and exploring yourself. When you grab that concept, life changes, and I say this with no condescension, last session we could have gone back down the ladder the other way. That was the epiphany moment for us. Now, the road ahead is yours to travel, no-peace or peace is up to you. Journey well.

Thanks, readers.

FINAL THOUGHTS

If you've read through this book without stopping, the first thing I suggest you do is go back and repeat the exercises. You'll learn more about yourself. Then place each of the exercises, or insights, somewhere into your life, even if it's just one exercise at a time. This way you can learn what works for you and what doesn't. This book is designed to stimulate your curiosity and start you on the road to change, not to give you all the answers. It's meant to get you to take a look at your life and see what answers you find for yourself. It's also a good idea to read more books on these subjects and talk to professionals, teachers, religious leaders, or those who have already found their own answers. Life is a process, not a destination. You must continually evolve, or you will dissolve. Think about it. If you're not improving, learning, or growing… what else can you do?

Anyway, I hope this book will stir up something in your life that says, "I'm capable of having more," or, "How can I change to make my marriage better," or, "How can I accomplish XYZ?" If I've at least gotten your juices flowing, then I feel I've at least done you some good. We are also working on several other books that will go into even more detail, as well as more specific topics. Additionally, I invite you to attend one of our workshops in person and experience everything I've talked about here in this book (and more!) for yourself. I also welcome any suggestions you may have for other books.

Please write me at:
TF@Architecting360.com

Any suggestions will be read and thoroughly reviewed. I wish I could give you all that the art of hypnosis and N.L.P. has given to me, but that's another book for another time (coming soon!).

Become a member of our AIT (Architects in Training) program or our main website www.TravisFox.net and enter your email address for a free e-book "Unwind Your Mind" and so much more. There's no cost at all and you get mailings throughout the year detailing our schedule, new webinars, videos and books, LIVE Events and Trainings & more.

I wish you all the joy & adventure as Spirit inside you, guides your heart and soul as it has touched mine. Thank you so much for your time, and remember, "It will be the most fun you'll ever have in your sleep!"

Travis Fox,

Printed in the United States
By Bookmasters